DEPRESSION SEX & DEATH

A Memoir

BY

TAMEISHA MOORE

ISBN-13: 978-0-692-76259-2
ISBN-10: 0-692-76259-0

Ordering Information:

Tamei2.wix.com/memesite

Acknowledgements

Special thanks to my mother for letting me use her poems.
Thanks to all my special friends who believed in me and
never judged me. Thank you to the people who donated to
my go fund me account God Bless you!

This book is for whoever suffers from depression, anxiety, or
any other mental illnesses. To those who have been in
abusive relationships, I say to you, BE STRONG, GET THE
HELP YOU NEED, AND NEVER LOSE FAITH. I have had
hard times, but I never lost my FAITH. God is Good!

Dedication

I dedicate this book to my Mother.

IN MEMORY OF:

Tiffaney Moore
Mable Brown Hamilton
Levell Law
Mary Savannah
Sam Foster

Table of Contents

INTRODUCTION

I'm sharing my story because it helped me as I wrote it. A catharsis of sorts that I hope affects someone else who is battling depression and anxiety. For the ones who self-inflict pain on themselves, I understand. A lot of people don't. I get it, but it's not good to self-harm. GET HELP! An abusive relationship is not love! I've come a long way, and I still have a long way to go. But definitely, where I'm at today is far better than where I was seven years ago. This Is My Story...

TEN

Ten was the age at which my life changed; for it was when I first experienced death and depression combined...

1997 was the year that changed everything for me. My oldest sister, at age fifteen, was a very loving, kind-hearted, and inspiring model. She was tall, skinny, and very pretty with long flowing hair as beautiful as she was kind.

She had many friends who loved her. She was just that type of person who was special from the time she was born until the time she died.

At ten, I would never have thought in a million years that I would lose someone so close to me, but I did.

Tiffaney had begun complaining of having pounding headaches that went on for several days to the point where her eyes would puff up, and my mother decided to take her to get it checked out.

While at the hospital, the doctor didn't take any blood or urine samples. They just simply assumed it was the flu and sent her home with pain medication.

When Tiffaney and my mom arrived home, Tiffaney was very high off the pain pill, so her head wasn't hurting as bad. Even though I was ten-years-old, I was still sleeping with my mom. I decided I would try sleeping on my own that night because my mom wanted Tiffaney to sleep with her so she could watch her.

Instead of sleeping in the bedroom I "shared" with Tiffaney, I crashed on the couch cause I didn't like sleeping in the room; being extremely close to my mother, guess that would make me a "mama's girl"... That night, I prayed and asked God to make my sister better before I fell asleep.

I'm still not sure what time it was, but it was sometime in the morning when I woke up and saw Tiffaney walking by the couch where I slept. My mom asked her where she was going, but she got no response.

As I watched her pass by, she had a frightening look on her face, but being that I was half asleep, I didn't pay it any mind and simply dozed back off. I don't know how long after, but I was startled awake by a noise, but assumed I was hearing things, so I didn't get up. Then there was a vivid sound; one I knew I should respond to, so I jumped up and walked towards our bedroom. I saw Tiffaney on our dresser in a sitting position, leaning back with her head to the side.

I called her name, but she didn't answer. She was labor breathing as if she was out of breath. Her nose was bleeding, so I ran to get my mom.

We got back to Tiffaney as quickly as we could, and immediately tried to stand her up, but at 6'1", she was just dead weight. She fell and began to have something similar to a seizure.

We didn't know what was happening to her. She didn't know either. I watched as a tear rolled down her face not knowing that would be her last tear. 911 was called, and they got there quick. I ran down the street to tell my other sister who was two years older than me. She was staying the night at her best friend's house the night before this happened. She wasn't far from our house. As I walked, I thought about what was happening. I'd had a gut-wrenching feeling in my stomach from the minute I saw her on that dresser.

When Tiffaney arrived at the hospital via ambulance, they ran all types of tests to find out what was wrong with her. They finally find out it was meningitis. Meningitis is inflammation of the brain and spinal cord membranes caused by an infection. But by the time they got the results, it was too late. Tiffaney was brain dead. I didn't really understand what being brain dead was at the time. I just knew I was going to tell her how bad it scared me to see her so sick. I thought I was going to have a chance to tell her how much I loved her and begged her to please not scare me like that again.

My mom kept her on life support for a week. Before Tiffaney got sick, she had been planning on going to a Military Ball on January the 17th. That's the day my mom let them take her off of life support. My mom and my dad were in the room as they took my big sister off the machine that was breathing for her. My mom held her until her heart stopped beating. Shortly after, my brother who was the eldest, but wasn't living with us at the time, came to me and said, "She's gone. She's gone MiMi." I began to cry. I couldn't believe, no, I didn't want to believe, what my brother was telling me. Tiffaney, my sister, was dead, and I would never see her again.

The fact that I couldn't tell her how much I loved her and that I wouldn't see her anymore was just too much for me. I was in total shock and disbelief. That was the saddest day for my family and me.

The next day, I was in the hospital for dehydration, and they ran tests on me to make sure I didn't have meningitis as well. They did a spinal tap, a procedure in which a needle is inserted into the spinal cord in order to remove some fluid for testing. This procedure could've saved my sister if only they would've done it when she first went to the hospital with a headache.

After I got out of the hospital and went home, it felt very different not seeing Tiffaney around the house. My mom cried a lot. She would sit in a rocking chair and just cry, and when she cried, we all cried.

For my sister's funeral, my mom pressed Tiffaney's hair and did her makeup. I know that was probably the hardest thing my mom ever had to do, but she wanted to do it. I couldn't imagine combing my daughter's hair as she laid in a casket. My mom is a very strong person, though, and with God and Xanax pills, that she took for her anxiety, she got through it.

The day of Tiffaney's funeral, I was still in disbelief that she was gone. She had a lot of family and friends, and the church was full. I was just numb still not really understanding that my sister is dead and how she looked as if she was sleep laying in the casket still beautiful.

The weeks after Tiffaney's funeral were the hardest as family and many so-called friends faded away. I would watch as my mom would lay Tiffaney's clothes on her bed and just cry. It was very depressing to see how hurt she was. I hated seeing her cry, so I would just cry, too. I believe my depression started when Tiffaney died because I didn't know how to deal with losing someone I loved so much. It was very hard, and I missed half of fifth grade that year. I started seeing a counselor a month after she had passed. I blamed myself at times with reasons like "if only I would've gotten up when she walked into the living room" or "if only

I wouldn't have fallen back asleep". There were a lot of "what ifs".

I cried a lot at my Counselor's office. It was hard talking about it. I blamed God too, for not answering my prayers. I had prayed that night before I went to sleep. At ten, I thought once you pray about it, God was supposed to answer your prayers, but He didn't answer my prayers. And I was mad that He didn't heal my sister and that He let her die. I felt like my sister should've still been alive, and it was God's fault that she wasn't. I was ten, and I thought like a ten-year-old. Now, I know it wasn't God's fault my sister died. That's just how it was meant to be. Tiffaney was a sick child, so God didn't want her to have to suffer any longer.

Only with time did things begin to get better, or rather easier to the point where the hurt wasn't on the surface. Time heals everything. My mom stopped crying as much, and I started going back to school. I still saw a Counselor as things began getting better for my family.

I still miss my sister very much, and not a day goes by that I don't think of her. I will forever love Tiffaney!

This is a poem my mother had written for Tiffaney before she was born!

"Your Own World"

My little baby in a world of your own

From the time you were conceived

I can feel how you've grown

The tiny little flutters are now

Strong movements and kicks

What are you doing in there?

It feels like summersaults and tricks

At times I wonder if you

Are doing alright

When I don't feel well

Or can't sleep all night

Precious little baby I long to

Hold you in my arms

To love and protect you

And keep you from all harm

Whether you are a boy or girl

Tameisha Moore

It is not known

For you little baby

Are in a world of your own

Love, Mommy

February 21, 1981

A poem written by my mother one year after Tiffaney's Death.

"In Loving Memory of Tiffaney Darleen Moore"

A year has passed since I saw your

Beautiful Smile

And just to see your face again

I'd walk 1,000 Miles

I'll keep your smile within my heart

Until we meet again

I miss you Tiffaney, so very much

My daughter and my Friend

Love, Mom

Tiffaney passed away January 17th, 1997. It's been 18 years, and I still miss her as much as I did back then.

I think about her a lot and wonder how it would be if she were still alive. I wonder what she would be doing and would she be a model or a singer; I wonder how she would be with her nieces and nephew and would she have kids of her own.

I wonder a lot about how it would have been...

TWELVE-YEARS-OLD

I know you are probably wondering what happened to me at the age of twelve. Twelve is the age at which I lost my virginity to a sixteen-year-old. Crazy, I know, but it happens. At twelve, I didn't know what I was doing, I was too young to know, but I did think I was in love with this boy. He was my first in many ways. My first love, the first boy I had sex with, and the first person to abuse me.

I saw him around the neighborhood often and had been attracted to him from the moment I had laid eyes on him. There was something about him, and I wanted to get to know this boy that I was always seeing. Eventually, we started talking, and then we started "kicking it". I knew he frequented the basketball court, and I would make sure when I saw him heading that way, I would go up there, too. We would talk. I would let him feel on me, and we would kiss before I had to go in the house. I'm talking about the days where your mom didn't want you to be outside once he street lights were on. I would kiss him goodbye, go home and think about him all night while hoping to see him the next day. Sometimes I did, but I hated it when I didn't. I don't know why I liked him so much, but in my 12-year-old mind, he was everything. It was Puppy Love…

We had been talking for some months when I decided to have sex with him. The day I went over to his house, he was home alone. I was so nervous and scared. He walked me to his room, and first we talked. Then we started kissing. He began to pull my pants and panties off. He laid me down on the bed and then laid next to me as he put a condom on. He slowly got on top of me and tried to enter me. It wasn't easy. I was so tight due to being a virgin. He kept trying, and it finally it went in. It hurt badly. I simply couldn't take the pain, and I made him stop. I didn't know what to expect, but I wasn't expecting it to be so painful. After I had made him stop, I put my clothes on and left to go to my friend's house. I went to the bathroom and found a little blood in my panties. I was so damn scared, and my vagina was hurting, but I couldn't tell anyone, so I just dealt with it.

After that, it took a couple of weeks before he was able to talk me into doing it again. I was weak-minded over this boy. He had such control over me. I was still a child, so whatever he said, I would do. I would lie to my mom and say that I was at a friend's house around the corner, but I would actually be with him. I would do whatever it took just to be with him, including lying to my mother. Everyone in the neighborhood knew about the boy and me. They knew I was his girl and that I was crazy about him. We got along well until I started making him mad by talking to other dudes behind his back. Guys were always trying to talk to me when I would walk to my friend's house. I guess I didn't look as young as I actually was. I lied about my age to a couple of guys. I thought about telling them my real age, but I knew they wouldn't talk to me if I did.

By the time I was thirteen, I had started messing with a dude named Chris even though I was still seeing the boy from the basketball court. We would talk on the phone, or he would come see me at my friend's house. I left with him one day not knowing my boyfriend saw me. I called my boyfriend once I made it back, and he was upset with me and called me all types of names. I realized I had messed up. The next day, I tried to see him. He wouldn't talk to me, and he pushed me. I was begging for him to forgive me and swore that nothing had happened with Chris and me and that I would never lie again. I had, in fact, cheated with Chris a lot of times. I wasn't trying to hurt anyone. I was just doing something – anything – that would take my mind off my sister. I was using sex as my escape from everything. I had been through a lot. Trying to deal with losing my sister and my depression was hard. Sex helped me in a way. I never got pleasure from sex at that age, just pain, but it took my mind off my other pain.

While my boyfriend and I were still seeing one another, my grandmother got sick. She had been sick on and off. My mom was the one taking her to her doctor's appointments. She had been going back and forth to see her doctor for a while, and it took them a while to find out what was wrong with her.

I would go to my grandmother's house and help her, walk her down the hall, and feed her peaches. She was getting so weak, and we didn't know what was wrong with her.

She had gotten so sick that she started throwing up feces. They found out she had a blockage and needed surgery, immediately. If that wasn't enough of a dose of bad news, they did the surgery and found cancer in her body. They did such extensive surgery that she had to have a colostomy bag. While my grandmother was sick, my mother tried to care for her while being in school herself and caring for her own kids. During this time, I was still messing with my boyfriend. We were still having sex, but I was only doing it for him. My mom had no idea I was having sex at such a young age especially with a sixteen-year-old boy. Something was wrong with that picture, I know, but I was vulnerable. I had been through a traumatic ordeal two years before, and he took advantage of me. I was too young to see that I was but a child. Yes, I wanted him, and yes, I wanted to have sex with him, but I was twelve, and I had a twelve-year-old mind. He was sixteen and having sex with a twelve-year-old girl, so yes, he took advantage of me.

May the tenth was my grandmother's birthday. We headed to the hospital with her presents and was stopped by my little cousin. His first words to us were "she dead". The way he said it pissed me off. He was young, so we didn't believe him and continued to her room. That's when we were told that yes, she had indeed passed away. I was in shock. I couldn't believe my grandmother was gone. She was the one who had done everything right. She lived for God and was a very good Christian lady. When she would answer her phone, she would say, "Hello, praise the Lord." My grandmother couldn't be dead, but I could see her just lying there as if she were sleep. I couldn't even cry I was so stunned.

My aunt arrived, and when she saw her mother, she was in disbelief. She kept looking at her, trying to see if she was breathing. I had to leave the room when I began laughing uncontrollably. I couldn't stop laughing! I'm not sure why except that maybe I guess it was to keep from crying.

On the way home was when it hit me that my grandmother was really gone. I cried so hard. When I got home, I just sat on the porch and cried. It had only been three years since my sister had died.

My mother was beyond sad; she loved her mother with every fiber in her body. She had so many pressures already with school and family responsibilities. Her mother's death was another weight added to the shoulders of her world…she was still taking the Xanax, which helped a lot with dealing with the death of her mother. She was so hurt, the same hurt she felt when my sister died.

***

After my grandmother's funeral, we ended up moving into my grandmother's house. I didn't want to at first, but my boyfriend stayed right down the street, so he was closer to me.

He was in and out of jail the whole time we were dating. My mom still didn't know about us until one night when he beat me up in the back of my friend's car. When we got to his house, he tried to drag me out of the car to get me in the house; the only thing that saved me that night were some girls who had come to his house, and I was able to leave. I was crying, scared, and in shock that this boy that I thought loved me would hurt me so badly.

Once home, I didn't say anything to anybody. I couldn't stop crying, so I got a razor and cut myself. When my mom asked what was wrong with me, I could only cry in response. When she saw the blood on my hand, she rushed me to the hospital. That's when the truth came out about me losing my virginity to a sixteen-year-old at twelve. At this point, he was eighteen, and I was going on fourteen.

The doctor asked me so many questions about what had happened that night and why I cut myself. They wanted to know how long this boy and I had been messing around. I wasn't trying to get him in trouble. I mean, yes, I was young, but I had laid there and opened my legs to him even though I didn't really know any better. I thought I was in love, and I was still trying to protect him.

My mom was very upset about the boy hitting me and causing me to damn near have a nervous breakdown. She was beyond mad. She made a police report about him beating me up and sleeping with me. With my mom's discovery came the end of the boy and me. I would still talk to him behind her back sometimes, but like I said, he was always in and out of jail. This was actually a good thing because I knew then that I didn't need to be messing with him.

Having sex at such a young age had opened up a Pandora's box of sex, abuse, and low self-esteem for me. Sex became my escape from reality. Having sex with a sixteen-year-old and being abused by him seemed like a normal enough relationship in my young mind.

TEENAGE YEARS

My teenage years were when I became really promiscuous. In high school, I thought if you slept with a lot of boys, you would be popular. I had no idea they would call you a "hoe".

I was fourteen when I got drunk for the first time. My good friend and I went to a house party with her cousin. We were really drunk! I guess we got so drunk because it was our first time drinking. We ended up passed out, and all I remember was waking up with a dude who I didn't know on top of me. Another dude was on top of my friend. I didn't know if we'd had sex or not as I was too drunk to recall. We found out days later that the boys had indeed had intercourse with my friend and I. We didn't even know their names, but they knew ours.

How can someone have sex with a person who was pissy drunk? I would call that rape, but we were young and didn't care enough to tell anybody what happened. They probably wouldn't have believed us just because we were drunk. It still wasn't right for them to sex us when we were too drunk to say no. We were passed out and couldn't remember much from that night.

We heard people around school saying we had gotten drunk and let the boys have sex with us. No one realized that we didn't let them. They had taken it that night.

In high school, my three friends and I would get together on the weekend, tell my mom a good lie, and go somewhere to get drunk and high. Once we got full of liquor, we would call the boys over to wherever we were and "get fucked" as we called it, and as it's stilled called that today.

Getting drunk and getting fucked was our routine. We were crazy girls. I remember one time we were all in a closet at my sister's boyfriend's house while they weren't there. We got fucked in that closet. We did some crazy shit, my girls and I. The boys from school were always trying to see what we had planned for the weekend and what we were drinking so they could come over.

One weekend, we were over at my brother's house drinking, and we got drunk. One of my friends and I went into my brother's bathroom and got fucked. When my brothers' wife found out, they put our asses out. They said we had to go. It was a while before I went back over there.

My girls and I knew we all slept with the same boys. Hell, we didn't care. We were just having fun.

During the time we were having all this fun, I met a boy. He was friends with my sister's boyfriend. He liked me, and I liked him, so we didn't wait long to have sex. We had sex everywhere, even outside. He wasn't my boyfriend, though. We were just fooling around. I did like him, but I wasn't looking for a boyfriend. My girls and I were too busy having fun.

God has a way of slowing you down, and He slowed me down at sixteen when I found out I was pregnant!

I couldn't believe I was pregnant. I had missed my period, so I took a pregnancy test. Two lines are what I saw. I remember thinking, Damn, I don't want to have a baby. I wasn't ready. When I found out I was pregnant, I already knew who I was pregnant by because, at that time, I was only sexing Jeff.

When I told Jeff I was pregnant, his words to me were, "You're not having it." I was like, Cool. I didn't want a baby.

I began to have morning sickness and terrible headaches. My mom would ask me what was wrong with me. I would just say that I didn't feel well, and when I would throw up, I would say I'd caught a virus. I would lie and say my cycle was on. I was lying about everything because I didn't want my mom to know I was pregnant.

My plan was to get an abortion, but I wasn't working, so I didn't have the money. Jeff never came up with the money, so before I knew it, months had gone by. I was still telling my mom that I didn't know what was wrong with me. I was still sick and throwing up.

My sister knew, but she wanted me to actually tell my mom. At first, I refused, but then I told my mom the truth. She said that she already knew and had just been waiting for me to tell her. She did ask me what I wanted to do. I had initially wanted an abortion, but I then decided to have the baby. My mother was hurt that her sixteen-year-old child was going to have a baby. Then she looked at the brighter side and was happy this would be her first grandchild.

Weeks later, I started going to the doctor. That's when found out the baby was a boy. I was happy because I didn't want a girl. I was still going to school too. I knew people were talking about me, but I didn't let that worry me. Around my fifth or sixth month, I had to switch to homeschooling because the baby was sitting on one of my nerves, and it had become very hard for me to walk. The teacher would come to the house with my work. I would do my assignments and turn them into him.

I stayed sick throughout my whole pregnancy and had to go to the hospital a lot. I didn't think pregnancy would be like that. I watched my body change once I started to gain weight. It was very depressing, and I just couldn't wait until it was over. I had my son on February 12, 2004. He was a healthy baby boy who weighed in at 7lbs even.

After my son was born, I changed a lot. I was a mom. didn't do too much hanging with the girls or drinking anymore. I had this baby boy to look after with the help of my mom.

Around this time, my mom and I weren't getting along so well. She had a hysterectomy, and she was tripping with her hormones being out of balance. She and Jeff's people weren't getting along either. She cussed them out; Jeff cussed her out, and it was just a messy situation.

My son and I would stay the night with Jeff at his mom's house sometimes. I thought we were going to be together, but it wasn't working out. My mom decided to make him pay child support. She was able to do this since I was only seventeen. That's what ended the relationship between Jeff and me. He stopped talking to me for a while. He was mad at me, I know. We would still mess around from time to time, but the relationship was over. I was sad about it, but life went on.

After Jeff, I dated on and off, and I had friends, but nothing became serious. I would babysit for my sister to earn money until I found a job. Having a baby at a young age was hard, but my mom helped me out a lot as is expected from a wonderful mom.

EIGHTEEN

I was eighteen when I had my first abortion. There was a boy I had begun messing around with. I met him when we were going to parties at NSU. My friends went to college there, so we would go out there to party.

We would start out drinking on our hour-long drive to the parties. It never failed that we would have to use the restroom on our way there. We would have to pull over and pee on the side of the road.

That night, in particular, I was drunk and dancing. I saw this handsome dark-skinned boy checking me out. I was checking him out, too. We danced together, and that's how we started talking. He was attending school in Natchitoches I made sure to attend most parties they had out there because I had to see him. When I would go, I would stay the night, and we would have sex and talk. He would come home on the weekend and pick me up. We would sometimes have sex at his house when his mom wasn't there, or we would go somewhere and do it in his car. I was always ready to get sexed.

My attitude began changing, and my breasts were sore, but pregnancy never popped into my head. Then my sister mentioned that I had been in a bad mood and asked if I was pregnant. I told her no. Shortly after that, I missed my cycle. I asked him if he had ejaculated inside me, and he said, "Yes". I started to cry because then I knew I was pregnant again. I was disappointed in myself and mad at him for not telling me what he had done. I told him that I wasn't ready for another baby, my son had just turned one and that there was no way I was keeping it. I made sure I kept it from my mom this time. No one knew other than my sister and two of my friends. I had to figure out where I was going to get the money from to have the abortion.

I cried a lot, and I became depressed again. I just couldn't see myself with another baby. My sister gave me half of the money. The father's mom gave him the other half. They even asked for a receipt! I thought it was crazy, but I didn't really care. They could have the receipt; I just couldn' have this baby.

The day of my abortion, I was terrified. I didn't know what they were going to do or how it was done. All I knew was that I was scared and wondering if I would go to hell for this. But I felt like I had to do it, so I did. My sister picked me up after the procedure was done. I fell asleep, and when I woke up, I felt so much better. The nausea was gone.

It was months later after the abortion, and Chad and I still messed around when he came in town, but I made sure he withdrew so that I wouldn't get pregnant again. I liked Chad a lot, but he was a player. My friends that went to school with him told me how he was messing with another girl, but when I would ask him about it, he would just lie to me. Then one day, the girl and I talked, and I found out that Chad had faked on me so hard. It was like I was nothing to him! He even said the baby wasn't his! I was so mad. If I could've found a ride to NSU, I would've hurt him. I just couldn't believe he would fake on me like that. After that, Chad and I went our separate ways.

SHUN

I started working at the Casino and Walmart. Before I started working there, I met a sweet boy named Shun. I saw him often at my home girl's house, and he would tell her that he wanted to holler at me. I figured it'd be okay to give him a try. He had a baby with someone else, but her and my home girl were friends. She wanted him to tell his child's mom that he had started dating me, and he did. He was one of the most real dudes I ever dated. He was so nice to me. We started spending a lot of time together when he wasn't sleeping. He would sleep late...very late. I would go to his mom's house to see what he had going on, and he would be knocked out. I met his mom and his dad, and I let my mom meet him. Soon, I was falling for him, and I believe he cared about me too.

While dating him, I started working two jobs, one at night and the other one during the day time. My son was with his grandparents a lot, so I didn't have to find a sitter.

Shun would keep my car at night when I went to my night job. I was cool with that. My mom didn't know, but I trusted Shun. We would talk at night while I was at work. There were a few times that he would pick me up late, and that really irritated me, but I never thought he was cheating because I knew he slept a lot.

Shun and I never had sex. He wanted to, but I wasn't ready. I know we would have eventually, though.

One day, we got into an argument, and we went the whole day without talking. By night, I was desperate for him to call me. I liked him, so I gave in and called, but there was no answer.

As I lay in bed, I got a call from my sister. She asked me if I'd heard what happened to Shun. I said, "No." She told me that he was dead. I didn't want to believe her and asked if I could call her back.

I called his mom's house, and that's when they told me he'd been shot. I started crying then went and told my mom. My mom and I went to his mom's house. His mom was so sad. I felt like I was dreaming and that this couldn't be real. I never got a chance to tell him I was sorry for arguing with him. We never got a chance to make up because now it was too late. I cried for days. I was so sad and missed him terribly. I took a week off from both of my jobs. It was hard losing a boyfriend. Even though Shun and I had only been together for a couple of months, I was still very sad.

His child's mother sat by me at his wake; she even put her arm around me and consoled me by saying that it was going to be alright. All I could do was cry. I had never seen my girlfriend cry, but that night she was crying hard. I felt so sorry for her too.

When Shun died, girls were coming from everywhere saying that they had been messing with him. I didn't care. It wasn't like I could ask him about it. His mother and father knew about me, and that's all that mattered. I'm sure he had friends, but I was his girlfriend when he died.

Shun was the youngest in his family. I hated that his mom had to bury a child. He was a good person who had a good heart.

I also hated that we never got a chance to make love, but that's how it was meant to be…

Depression, Sex and Death: A Memoir

***

A week after Shun's death, I went back to work. I cried a lot at work because I missed him so much. It was weird not having him driving me to my night job anymore. I think I worked for two more weeks, and then I let go of my night job. It just brought back too many memories.

Keeping my day job was better for me. I would still cry from time to time, but after a while, I met a man from at work, and that helped me get my mind off Shun.

He and I started talking. He was much older than me, but I liked him. He was cool, and I liked his swag. We started kicking it. The sex was good. I would go to his house late at night, we would have sex, and I would go home. At work, we would act like we didn't have anything going on, but I was very sexually attracted to him. We had sex a lot, but I realized later that he was just using me. He would ask me for money, and my dumb ass would give it to him. He would only have sex with me after I gave him oral sex. I had never been good at it, but I would do whatever he said because I liked him. I was so much younger than him. I didn't really think. I just did what he asked.

He ended up getting fired, but we would still meet and have sex but not a lot. Then we just stop talking completely. He did help me get over Shun's death, though.

TWENTIES

I had my first orgasm at age twenty. I met an older man named John while I was working. He was selling purses, and I bought one from him. After that, we began talking. He was so nice to me from day one. I was twenty years old; he had kids older than me, but I didn't care. I was feeling the old man because he was very nice to my son and me. My son loved the old man. My mom didn't care for him at first, but once she saw how he treated my son, she came around.

The old man John introduced me to sex toys. I told him I had never had an orgasm in my life, and he couldn't believe it! He told me we were going to try a particular sex toy and that if it didn't work then something was wrong.

I allowed him to introduce sex toys to me. At first, I didn't think it would work at all, but as he kept going, I started feeling something I had never felt in all the years I had been having sex. Oh my, it felt so good. I didn't know

41

what was happening. I grabbed his arm, and as I came, I started moaning. That first orgasm was the best feeling I'd had in my life. After that first orgasm, every time John and I would mess around, he had to use the sex toy. He even bought me one of my own, and I would make myself cum as he watched. The old man was turning me into a freak, but he was crazy about me. He would do or get whatever I said or needed. He even let me drive his Cadillac truck!

I cared about the old man, but I got so tired of people telling me shit about him like who he was talking to or trying to talk to. I tried to leave him alone, but he would cry like a baby, and I would take him back. He would act like he wasn't doing anything, but people would tell me that he had a woman he had been with for a long time. We never came across each other; he made sure of that.

He would show me off to his friends around his age. A lot of his friends tried to talk to me, but I was with the old man. He took care of me, so I couldn't do him like that. For my son's birthday, I know he spent about five hundred dollars on toys. He bought him so many toys that I didn't let him play with some of them for months because there were so many. The old man John was a sweetheart.

While I was dating him, I met another man at work; he was much older than me, and we hit it off. He was a very attractive, dark-skinned brother.

We started kicking it, and from there, we started having hot sex. As soon as I would walk in the house, he would push me against the wall and fuck me. He loved seeing me, and I loved seeing him. I did tell him about the old man, so when the old man would call, I would lie and say that I was at my girlfriend's house or something. I didn't want the old man John to find out, but I knew one day he would. I always felt as if he was watching me or had people watching me.

He wanted me all to himself, and for a while, he had me...until I met Anthony

Anthony and I messed around a lot, and the old man started to question my whereabouts. He never caught me, and that's all that mattered.

I turned twenty-one while I was with the old man John. I was finally able to go out to the clubs! The old man

John didn't like that because he knew dudes would be trying to holla at me, and they did. Around this time, me and Anthony had stopped messing around. I wasn't the finest, but I never had a problem getting a man. The club was where I met Mike. He'd had a girlfriend when we first started talking, but once we got serious, he broke up with her for me. Mike was cool, and I liked him. He had a mouth full of gold fronts. My first had a mouth full of gold too, so that had become something I was attracted to.

One night, I was dressed to kill. The old man had seen what I had on, and he waited for me outside the club that night. He wanted to make sure I didn't leave with anybody. I had planned on leaving with Mike. I was so drunk that night that all I remember was the old man John taking me to his house. I'm sure he had sex with me, but I had passed out. When I woke up, I decided to leave. He tried to make me stay, but I left anyway, and he followed me. Mike called me, and I told him to meet me at my mom's house. We all ended up at my mom's house. The old man started talking shit saying how we had just had sex. I couldn't remember if we had or not. The old man was being ı hater that night. He and Mike had words, but my mom :ame outside and told the old man to leave, and he did. √like and I talked until the sun came up.

The old man John was mad at me, and he cried. I lidn't care. I had this new dude giving me attention, so I was falling back from the old man. Mike and I developed a 'elationship. I told Mike I wasn't dealing with the old man ohn anymore. We weren't having sex, but I was still talking o him.

One morning, I was in the old man John's truck. Mike 1ad to go to work, so I told Mike that it was my uncle's truck ınd took him to work. I was very nervous that John would ind out, but he didn't.

The night I decided to stay with Mike for the first ime, the old man John called me at least one hundred times. He was out looking for me in Bossier. He thought I was with Anthony, the one I use to have hot sex with, but I wasn't. He :alled me all night. Morning came, and I left Mike's house to ;o to work. I got home, took a bath, got ready, and headed 'ight back out. All the while, the old man was still calling.

When I finally answered, he was talking shit to me, asking me where I was. I wouldn't tell him. I made it to work, and the old man pulled up right behind me still talking shit. He was saying that he wasn't going to give me my two thousand dollars back that I had let him borrow from my taxes that year. He was going to come in my job and tell everybody that I was a hoe. He was calling me all types of names. The whole time he was running his mouth, I was looking through my purse. Once I found what I was looking for, I maced his dumb ass. He parked that truck so fast and got out looking for some water. I walked right into work like nothing had happened. He shouldn't have come to my job with that mess. Once I got my money, I cut him off, and it was just Mike and me.

Mike wasn't good for me at all, but I fell for him. At first, things were cool. Until one rainy day as I was taking him to work, we got into it over something, and Mike slapped me! I could've wrecked! After that, I didn't say anything else. I was shocked beyond belief that he had done that. I dropped him off and went to work. He texted me like nothing had happened and didn't even try to apologize or othing. That was a sign that I should've left him alone, but I didn't. I kept talking to him, and months later, I found out I was pregnant with Mike's baby. He didn't want me to have the baby. I wanted to, but since he didn't want me to, I got an abortion when I got my taxes that year. Mike didn't give me a dime either. After a while, I got tired of him and decided to end it. I went to his house one night to tell him. He didn't want to hear it. He just wanted to know why I didn't want to be with him. I simply told him that I didn't want to be with him anymore. I got up to leave, and he pushed me so hard that I flew across the room. He took my keys and wouldn't let me leave; then he took my phone so that I couldn't call anyone for help. I was afraid of Mike. He only allowed me to leave the next morning because he had to go to work.

Mike and I stayed together. I don't know why because he didn't even trust me. People were always telling him something about me, though most of it was lies.

During the time I was with him, I met a boy named, Fred. I used to see him all the time around the neighborhood. Fred was tall and skinny with a head-full of hair. Fred told my girlfriend that he wanted to talk to me. I was interested, so when I would see him at her house, we would talk. He was a very sweet person, and I started liking him.

He would come by my mom's house and blow the horn as he drove by. I would be hoping it was him when I heard it, and when it was, it would put a big smile on my face. On days I didn't see Fred, I would ride around the neighborhood hoping to see him somewhere. Fred was my boo. Around the time Fred and I were talking, I was still with Mike. People would go back and tell Mike I was messing with Fred, but I would deny it.

At that time, my sister and I decided to get an apartment together. The day before we moved in, Fred stayed the night with me at my sister's house. We kissed and stuff, but we didn't have sex. We both wanted to, but my baby niece was in the bed, so we just laid down and went to sleep. When morning came, Fred gave me my half of the deposit.

The night we finished moving in, we went out to the club. My plans were to let Fred come over. He told me to make sure I called him when I left the club, but I couldn't because Mike made sure he came home with me that night. I didn't know how to tell Mike not to come over without him thinking I had other plans. So I didn't say anything at all. I thought about Fred the whole time, though.

The next day, Mike looked at my phone and saw that been talking to Fred. He got mad and punched me in the head. He choked me for about three minutes. This seemed like a very long time when you can't breathe. Somehow, I was able to get up and run to my sister's room. I couldn't even speak. I was just crying. He had choked me so hard that I couldn't talk for a couple of minutes.

My sister was asking what was wrong. I just couldn't tell her, but I know she knew Mike had done something to me.

I went back to my room, still crying. Mike apologized to me, and we had sex then went to sleep.

When I woke up, I was told that Fred had been shot and had died. I started crying again. I couldn't believe Fred was dead. I didn't want to believe that Fred was dead. Mike asked me what was wrong, and I told him. He didn't like the fact that I was crying over another man, but I didn't care. I cared about Fred. Mike then asked me to take him home, and I did.

After I had dropped him off, I called my friend that knew Fred and asked if it was true. She said that he wasn't dead but was in bad shape. He had been shot multiple times and they didn't know if he was going to make it. I was happy he wasn't dead, but scared he was going to die.

I was told that Fred had a girlfriend, so I didn't want to just pop up at the hospital. For days, I would just wonder how he was doing or call my friend for an update. I worried about him so much that I started dreaming about him. That' when I knew I had to see him for myself. My mom and I went up there, and I wasn't sure which room he was in, but somehow I found it. I went in not knowing if it was his room or not. I looked at his face, and when he opened his eyes, he started crying saying how he didn't want me to see him like that. He said that he wished I would've called him that night when I left the club.

Fred was messed up bad. He looked as if he had been hit by a car. He was in a full body cast. I felt so sorry for him

ut seeing him did make me feel a little better. I told him
hat people had been telling me not to come because he had
. girl. Fred told me not to worry and to come by and call
vhenever. Then he kissed me right in front of his girlfriend
nd told me he loved me! That made my day!

Fred lost his ability to walk due to the bone in his leg
aving been shot out. He was paralyzed, and his kidneys
vere messed up. He was in very bad shape. Right after Fred
vas shot, a lot of his family and friends visited, but after
ome months, most of the people, besides his family, faded
way. I stayed by his side, though. I went to see him every
lay, and I would take him food or whatever he asked me to
ring. I felt so sorry for this man. He had really started to
ffect me.

I hated seeing him like that and hated hearing him
ay that he wished he would've died that day. I would just
ell him that it wasn't his time and that God wasn't ready for
im to be with the Lord.

During all of this, I was still working. My sister and I
veren't getting along. Mike and I weren't either. I had so
nuch going on that I was stressed to the max. One day, I

went to work and just lost it. I couldn't stop crying, so my Manager sent me home. The devil wanted me to kill myself and told me to cut my wrist. Instead of cutting my wrist, I cut my hand. Cutting relieved my emotional pain. I told my mom, and she took me to the hospital. I was there for a week, severely depressed and suicidal. I was mentally and physically tired, and I wanted to die.

When I called Fred from the hospital and told him what had happened, he cried. We ended up crying on the phone together. He said that he wouldn't know how to take it if I killed myself. I just felt so bad for him, and I didn't know how to deal with it. My way of thinking was off in 2008. During my hospital stay, I was given medication and going to group therapy talking to other people that were there for all types of reasons. Some were there because they were alcoholics and others were there because they tried to kill themselves. It was people there that were hearing voices and some were there to detox. It was people there that I got close to because I understood what they were going through and they could relate to my problems. The food was nasty. We ate three times a day and dinner was at 6. After dinner, would be starving because there was nothing else to eat. You were not allowed to bring your own snacks or anything. When it was time for me to get released, they would give me a follow up appointment with the psychiatry and give me my prescriptions to get filled.

***

The year was 2008, and I had been in and out of the hospital for months because the medicine wasn't helping. They tried me on three or four different antidepressants and mood stabilizers. One mood stabilizer had me where I couldn't even think. It was like my mind went blank, so they had to take me off that. One day after I got out of the hospital, I overdosed. I just didn't care if I died, and I went back to the hospital and stayed a few days. I had to take a medical leave from work for a while so that I wouldn't lose my job.

While I was in and out of the mental hospital, I would go to group therapy and tell them why I was there and listen to why other people were there.

I noticed that most of the people there blamed their mother or father for their life being messed up. I couldn't blame my parents. I alone had made the decision to cut myself, take an overdose, and end up in the mental hospital.

During my hospital stays, the old man would come see me and sneak me gum and candy. My brother came, and my mom and a man I use to date would also visit me. I hated people seeing me in the hospital around all these mentally ill people. I looked just like the rest. They didn't even allow us to fix our hair. There were no mirrors, and combs weren't allowed.

It sucked being in the mental hospital, but during the times I was released, I would see Fred and Mike. I would do fine for days or maybe even weeks, but then that feeling of wanting to die would come back. It came back one day while I was at Mike's house. I tried to take an overdose again, but he took my pills and told my mom. Back to the mental hospital I went.

I was still very much depressed, and I couldn't shake it. In the hospital, when the patients and workers would get on my nerves, I would ask for my medicine early so I could go to sleep and not have to deal with anyone. Being in the hospital started making my nerves bad. They treated you

ike you were crazy and talked to you any kind of way. I
alked to my good friend one day, and she said it seemed
ike the hospital was only making me worse. I told her that I
:new I needed to get the hell up out of there.

The next time I got out, I stayed out maybe a month
or two. I ended up going back because Mike beat me up one
night. He had looked through my phone and didn't like
what he saw. I just laughed, and he threw the phone at me.
f I had not ducked, that phone would've hurt me. It was
broken into pieces. He hit me on my head. I tried to call my
.ister and 911 on another phone, but he took the phone and
nung it up. The police still ended up coming. They asked if I
nad called and was I alone. I never looked the police in their
'aces. I lied and said that I hadn't tried to call. They knew I
was lying, but they left.

After they left, I got a knife and started cutting
myself. Mike stopped me. He took the knife from me and
was telling me how much he loved me. We were both
:rying, and after that, we went and laid down.

When my mother found out what Mike had done, she was very upset, especially about him breaking my phone and hitting me. She really wanted to fuck Mike up.

I was admitted to the hospital yet again, but this time was different. I knew I had to get it together for real this time. I had to do the work, go to group therapy, take my medicine, but most of all, I had to pray. I prayed about it and told myself that this would be my last time there. When I got out, I started to feel like myself again.

I went back to the apartment where my sister and I had been living. I didn't have the rent money, but I still stayed there. When I did get money, I would buy food for the house.

This man I met when I was working was always trying to pay me to have sex with him. I went ahead and did it because I needed the money. Mike was broke, and I didn't want to keep asking my mom for money, so I only had sex with him for the money. The first time I slept with him, I was so nervous. I knew it was wrong, but all I was thinking about was the money. He would give me oral sex, and then we would do it. He was an older man somewhere in his ifties, so after only about fifteen minutes, he would come. I would get my five hundred and go.

I did this a couple of times with him until he started wanting sex more often. I couldn't be with him all the time. I had a boyfriend, and it started making me feel like a prostitute, so I had to break it off with him.

I only did it for the money. I had slept with so many guys for free all my life that I figured I might as well get paid for it. When Mike would ask where I got the money from, I would lie and tell him it came from my mom.

I was getting tired of Mike, so I started falling back from him. One day, I told him I wasn't in love with him, and he cried like a baby. I felt bad because I know he really did love me, but I was tired of him abusing me, being a bum, and not working. He didn't even have a car. I knew it was time to move on because I felt much better.

My sister was about to move somewhere with her husband, so I moved back home and finally went back to work. I had been on leave for four months; it was time to start back working.

When I went back to work, I found that they had hired a lot of new people. The new people thought I was new, too. They didn't know I had been there for two years.

Not long after I returned to work, I met a boy that worked in the same department as I did. I thought he was very tall and handsome. He asked for my number, and I gave it to him. He was a couple of years younger than me. I had never dated younger dudes, but there was something about him, so I gave it a try. We would get off at the same time, so I would invite him over to my mom's house. We would watch a movie and talk; then I would take him home He didn't have a car.

Most of the time, I would go see him, and the first time we had sex, it was great. I didn't expect much from tha little boy, but he fucked the shit out of me. I was hooked from that day forward. We couldn't resist each other. We would go on break at work and find somewhere to have sex and then return to work like nothing had happened.

The only way I could fuck him as much as I wanted was to get my own place, so I did. He would stay the night, and we would have sex all the time, almost every day. Then came the times when he would disappear, and I wouldn't hear from him for days. I would be sick with worry, and I would cry a lot. I couldn't understand why he would leave and not tell me anything. I even found out he was a cheater, but I didn't care. I wanted him, and I knew I would've done anything for that boy. He ended up getting fired from the job, so I would let him drop me off at work and keep my car. Did I trust him? No! But that little boy Dee had my mind gone.

His mother liked me, and I liked her. She was sweet, but she was no dummy. She knew her son was full of game.

He had a son, and one night while I was over at his people's house with him, the baby's mother came asking me questions. He beat the fuck out of her as if he didn't have a child with her. I felt sorry for her, but I wasn't going try to stop it. I didn't want him hitting me. His friends finally stopped it. I said to myself, this little boy Dee is crazy!!!

That was my sign that I needed to stop seeing him, but I didn't. I was too crazy over him. We would get into it, but he never hit me until one night we got into it, and I threw Kool-Aid on him. I was talking shit when he came up and hit me right in my face by my nose. I tried to call the police, but he took my phone, so I ran to the bathroom. When I looked at my face, I had a big knot on it. I started crying. I had the door locked, but he was knocking and saying he was sorry. I opened the door, and when he saw my face, he hugged me and apologized again. My dumb ass believed him. We went and laid down because I had to go to work the next day.

When I got up, I saw that I had a black eye. I knew that when my mom saw it, she was going to flip out. I still went to work, though. My coworkers wondered what had happened. I just told them that I'd had a fight.

Two days after he blacked my eye, I had to go to my mom's house for something. I tried to keep her from seeing my eye, but she saw it anyway. When she did, she did a double-take and said, "WHAT HAPPENED TO YOUR EYE??!!!!" She was pissed when I told her what happened. She called the police herself, and I went ahead and did a police report. I didn't have a choice. After that, I stopped talking to him. I missed him like crazy, and my eye was black for two weeks.

I would still see Fred, though not as much. He was in the hospital right around the corner from where I stayed, so some nights, I would go see him on the way home.

I knew I had to stop seeing Fred so much. I let his condition affect me too much, but I was always thinking of him. I told him about the little boy Dee. He didn't like the fact that I had been given a black eye.

Dee and I were off and on after the incident. One minute he would be there, and the next minute he would be gone for days. Even though I was crazy about him, I would fuck other dudes during the times he disappeared. Most of them would be dudes I had messed with in the past.

My black eye wasn't the worst thing he did to me, though. I noticed that I had begun losing money. This went on for about a month. I then started to suspect the boy was stealing from me. I didn't want to believe it, but I then found out he was. That broke my heart because he should have known that all he had to do was ask. If I had it to give, I would have given anything to him with no questions. I confronted him about it, but there was no denying it. I was so hurt.

Later that day, my brother and his friend came by. I can't remember why. After they left, my brother's friend came back. He was someone I had known nearly all my life. I was hurt and stressed, and I fucked my brother's friend that night. He replaced the money the little boy Dee had stolen from me with interest. We both said that my brother could never found out, and I didn't tell a soul about us being together. After that, we didn't talk for a while, and I was cool with that. He had given me what I needed that night, sex and money.

I stopped talking to the little boy for a while. I was still hurt and mad at him. During the time we were not talking, I met a white boy. He was so sweet to me. He was eight years older than me, but he didn't look like it at all. In fact, he looked younger than I did. We hit it off well. He took me on actual dates. My first time ever going to a strip club was with him. I let him talk me into going. He would come over, and we would chill and watch a movie. Both my sister and my mom liked him. He was a very likable person.

I didn't quite know what to expect the first time we had sex, but it was good. It was strange having sex with a white person. I don't know why exactly, but it was just weird to me. I liked him, so I looked passed my issue with that. He said he liked me, and I was feeling him too, but I still had feelings for the little boy Dee. I knew if the little boy called, I would push the white boy away. And I'll be darned if that the little boy didn't call. I told him I was messing with the white boy. He didn't like it.

We were broken up, but the little boy Dee had it in his mind that I wasn't supposed to talk to anyone but him. So when the little boy wanted to come over, I let him. I couldn't stay away from him even though I knew he was no good for me. Toxic is what he was. The night the little boy came over, he told me how much he missed me, that he was sorry, and how I had to let the white boy go. I said okay, but I wasn't going to stop talking to the white boy completely. After we had finished talking, we had sex and were about to go to sleep when I got a text from the white boy. Then he started calling. I couldn't answer the phone, so I hit the reject button each time he called. About twenty minutes later, I heard someone knock on the door. My heart dropped because I knew it was the white boy. I was so nervous because the little boy Dee was crazy. He started demanding to know who was knocking on my door that late. I said I didn't know, so he jumped up to put his pants on and answer my door.

I didn't even want to see what was about to happen because I knew the little boy Dee was going to be talking shit. He opened the door and asked the white boy who he was looking for. The white boy said, "MiMi." Now, I can't remember if he punched the white boy in the face first or what really happened next because it was all a blur. I ran to see what was going on, and the little boy was trying to pull the white boy into my house. I asked what he was doing, but they ignored me. The white boy was trying his best not to be dragged into the house, but the little boy overpowered him. Then the little boy pulled a gun on the white boy and took his watch and whatever else he had of value. I was in such shock that the little boy Dee did all that to my white friend. After being robbed, the white boy left.

Shortly after that, he and his friends started calling. They thought I had set him up. I tried to explain that I couldn't have set him up because he was the one who had

ust popped up. The white boy was mad, though, and kept
alling me names and shit. It pissed me off because I knew I
nadn't set him up, and I had no control over the FOOL that
nad answered my door. The white boy told me that he and
nis friends would be coming back, but I didn't really believe
nim. Dee and I laid back down. We laid there probably
hirty minutes, and he must have felt some type of way
necause he went outside. I called my good friend and told
ner what had just happened and now I'm thinking because
of this bullshit, I will be the one to end up getting shot. Not a
minute later, I heard gunshots. I was sitting on my bed, and
he shots came right by where I was sitting. They missed me
only because of GOD! I should have been shot! That bullet
ould've hit me through my left side or in my back, but
GOD saved me! I hit the floor and crawled to my son's
oom.

Thank God my son wasn't there. Neither one of them
gave a damn about me, my life, or my son's life because the
vhite boy didn't know if my son was there or not. He was
ust out for revenge. I hung up the phone with my friend.
he didn't know if I was shot or not. The little boy was

outside, and I just knew I was going find him lying on the ground. I started calling his name, and he came in from the back of my house. I was so damn scared. I didn't know what to do. My friend that I had been on the phone with hurried over. She was scared something had happened to me, but I told her I was okay. The bullets had gone right passed me. I called and told my sister what happened, and she came over too. It was early in the AM when all this went down.

My sister was mad at the little boy, and I was too because none of this should've happened. The little boy was wrong for what he did, and the white boy was wrong for coming back and shooting at my house. I had to call the police. I was too scared that they were going to come back.

When the police came, we couldn't tell them that the little boy Dee robbed him because he was a felon and wasn't supposed to own a gun. The white boy was a felon too. I knew this meant that somebody was going to go to jail. I just didn't know who or when. The police wrote up the report, and I gave him the white boy's name. I didn't want to, but considering he had almost shot me, I thought it was only fair.

I went to work later that day. I was still shaken up and crying a lot, so I left. Later that evening the little boy Dee came over. I cried on his shoulder. I was just scared for the two of us. He reassured me that everything was going to be alright, but I didn't think the problem would go away so quickly.

Days later, I talked to the white boy, and I told him that I didn't set him up. Once he saw that I was for real, he apologized. I sent him pictures of my headboard and told him that I had been sitting right where the bullets came through. He felt bad, and I started feeling bad because I had told the police his name. I guess that's what happens when you try to be a PLAYER!!!

When things were all sorted out, both of my boys ended up going to jail. The little boy was at the wrong place at the wrong time, and a gun was found. The white boy went for shooting at my house. I hated it for both of them, but I knew one day it was going to come back around on them.

I cried when the little boy Dee went to jail. I cared about him a lot. I would put money on my phone and go see him. One day I went to see him, and while I was there, I saw the white boy. I wasn't talking to the white boy anymore, though. The little boy Dee and I talked at least three times a week, and I would see him once a week. I did miss him, but mostly I missed the sex. I went a couple of months without sex while he was in jail, but I did slip up and have sex with my homeboy. It was just a one-time thing. Shit happens! After my homeboy, I wasn't interested in anyone else, and the little boy Dee and I stopped talking as much.

TEXAS

About four months after the little boy went to jail, I
started thinking about moving to Texas. At this time, it was
just a thought. I did decide to move back in with my mom so
I could start saving up some money. I didn't really want to
move back home because I loved being in my own place, but
it was what I needed to do. My mom and I got along well
after I moved back in. I would go to work and go home. I
wasn't messing around with anyone at the time. I had a
friend who lived in Texas, and she was trying to get me to
move out there. I started looking into whether or not I could
transfer my job. I found that I could, so I put in a transfer
and started looking for an apartment out there. My friend
helped me out a lot because she knew the area well. I sent
her my money for my deposit, and she went and paid it. My
transfer got approved. I prayed about it and made the
decision to step out on faith. I let my son stay with my father
in Texas until I got myself situated. My son left first, and I

left home about a week later. I was scared at first, but I had prayed about it and knew I needed to leave Shreveport.

Everything had fallen into place. I was going to be staying with my friend for two weeks until my apartment was ready. We got along well, and my brother stayed about twenty minutes away, so I would go over there sometimes. I can honestly say that I was happy. I had a peace of mind, and I wasn't stressing. I was just happy. My job was right up the street from where I was going to be staying. I couldn't be more grateful.

One weekend, my friend and I decided to go out, and we had a good time. While we were out, I ran across a dude that had tried to talk to me in Shreveport. I didn't talk to him long. There was something about him I didn't like, and I probably shouldn't have given him my number. My home girl reminded me of what I had said about the dude, but I still gave him my number. He hit me up as soon as he left the club. From that night, we talked every day. He didn't stay in Texas. He lived in Shreveport.

A couple of weeks later, I had to go to Shreveport and get the rest of my things. While I was there, Red and I spent

me time together, and he seemed alright. I wanted him to
me back with me to spend a couple of days out there, but
hen it was time for me to leave, I had no answer from him.

My girlfriend knew of Red. When I told her I was
lking to him, she said something I should've listened to.
he said, "Friend, just don't put your heart into it." If I
ould've listened to her, I could've saved myself from a lot
f heartache and drama. I didn't listen, and Red ended up
oming out there. It started out good. He was sweet at first,
ut I would see a different side of Red when he would drink.
hat's when he would start tripping and talking shit.

One night in the club, he pulled me by my hair. I can't
ven remember why, but that liquor would change him.
hat same night, Red threw drink all in my hair, my eyes,
nd all over my clothes. He had no reason to do that!

That night, I watched him do a line of coke up his
ose. I had never even been around a person that did coke. It
ripped me out, and he was talking shit to me over nothing,
ut I didn't say anything. I didn't want him to beat me up
while he was on powder. I had all the signs that I needed to
eave Red alone, but I didn't. Around my family, you

would've thought he was the perfect guy, but I knew he wa
putting on. I wasn't telling them the truth about him either.

Red and I would come to Shreveport on my off days
almost every week. I hated it. I only did it for him. That's
where his money was, so he had to go back and forth. I like
being in my apartment chilling on my days off, but that onl
happened a couple of times. I was working, and Red wasn't
and it would piss me off so bad when he would want to
leave to go Shreveport as soon as I got off. He wanted me to
drive most of the time, too. We would get into it over the
driving. I would be tired, and this dude would be at home
relaxing all day until I got off. I learned quickly how selfish
Red was. He would make me mad, then apologize, and buy
me something, and that's how he had me.

While we were in Shreveport, I would stay at my
mom's house because he would be in my car doing
whatever he did while we were here. Sometimes we would
get a room when we were in town, because I didn't want my
mom to know I was in Shreveport. Sometimes it felt like I
still lived in Shreveport because I was always there. I got so
tired of going there, but it was for Red.

About four months after Red and I got together, I
ided up becoming pregnant. I didn't want another baby,
nd I definitely DID NOT want one with Red. I was scared
) tell my mom, but I had to realize that I wasn't a little girl
nymore. I told her I was pregnant, but that I wasn't going
) have it. I was so sick. All of this happened around
hanksgiving, so I had to take a leave from work until I got
ie abortion. It was very hard for me to work pregnant.
Vhen I took the leave from work, I spent most of my time in
hreveport on my mom's couch sick. I couldn't get the
bortion at the time because I didn't have the money, so I
iad to wait until I got some. Red didn't have any money
ither. I was just pregnant and waiting.

Before I knew it, it was almost Christmas. My son was
till in Texas with my dad. My mom wanted me to get my
on, but I was so sick that I knew the drive was going to kill
ie. Yes, I wanted to see my son, but I was feeling so bad,
ind Red wouldn't go with me. I had no one to go with me,
o my mom asked the old man I used to date, and he said
es. We left out early the next morning. We didn't do too
nuch talking. He got us there safely, I got my son, and we

headed back to Shreveport. I never told Red. I let him think went by myself. I was grateful that the old man did that because he didn't have to. I didn't have any money to get my son's gifts for Christmas, but Red and my mom both bought my son some things, so he still had a good Christmas.

I still wasn't feeling well at Christmas, but I tried to keep up a happy face. My son's daddy and his family wanted to see him. I didn't want him to go. I just had a bad feeling! But my mom said that I should let him go, so I did.

A couple of days later, it was time for Tra to go back to school, so I told his daddy to bring him home. He told me that my son wasn't going back with me. I was very upset, so my mom and I went to the sheriff's office and told them what was going on, but they told me there was nothing I could do. He was the daddy, and I couldn't take him from him.

I knew I shouldn't have let him go with them. I had a feeling they were going to pull this shit. I couldn't do anything but go back home, call my daddy, and tell him Tra would not be coming back. My daddy was very upset. Tra

as doing well out there in school, and he had made a lot of
iends, but I couldn't do anything. I didn't have full custody
f my son. If I did, then I could've gotten him back.

I stayed in Shreveport longer than I planned, stressed
ut, and waiting until I could file my taxes so I could have
ome money to get the abortion. My mom offered to give me
he money, but my mom had already done so much for me,
o I told her I would wait until I got my taxes. As soon as my
ax return came in, I made me an appointment. At my first
ppointment, they took blood, checked to see how far along
was, and verified my blood type. Once that was done, they
cheduled my appointment to come back and get the
rocedure done. My appointment was three days later. Red
ook me and dropped me off. Red was mad because he
idn't want me to get an abortion, but I didn't want a baby
y him at all. They gave me some medicine to help me relax
nd to cause my cervix to start opening. I waited about
hirty minutes for the medicine to kick in. While I was
vaiting, I cried. I didn't want to kill another baby, but I
idn't want a baby by Red. I felt really bad. A part of me
vanted to get up and leave, but I had already taken the pills.

I was too high to go, and I was still crying. When my name was called, I was so nervous, but it was too late to turn around. Here goes nothing, I thought.

I went to the room where they do the procedure. I laid on the table, the nurse put a mask on my face, and she told me to take a deep breath. I started dozing off and on. My legs were wide open, and I started feeling pressure in the lower part of my stomach. Then I felt as if life got sucked right out of me. It was a feeling I really can't explain in a way other than that. Then, it was over. I asked God to forgive me, and I felt that He did. They told me to get up and go in the recovery room because they wanted to watch me for about an hour.

After an hour, they called my ride and told them I was ready. Red came and got me. I was so high; I really can't remember the ride home. I just remember lying on the couch and going to sleep, and I heard a knock at the door. My mom had sent the next door neighbor to check on me to make sure I was alright.

When I got up, blood started running down my legs and all on the carpet. I went to the bathroom and found that e pad I had on was full of blood. I called my mom. I didn't now what was happening, but I thought I was going to leed to death. My mom rushed home from work and called he place where I'd had the abortion. She told them what was going on, and they told her to watch me and for me to hange my pad. If it filled up in an hour, she was to take me ack. Thank God, it didn't. Not only was I very scared, but hy mom was also.

I laid back down on the couch. Red was still there. He buched my stomach, and he cried. He hadn't wanted me to lo that, but it was over and done with. Then he got mad and eft.

I stayed in Shreveport for a couple of days; then it was time for me to go back to Texas and go back to work. I was feeling better.

I went back to work, and everything got back to hormal. Red was still getting on my nerves, stressing me out. He talked to me any kind of way, and he was cheating. I would look at his phone and see that he was always talking o girls. He would swear up and down that he wasn't cheating even though I knew he was lying. Red and I stayed into it. He was always tripping with me about something. He was still going back and forth to Shreveport. Sometimes he would ride the bus, and I would have to take him to the bus stop. Afterward, I would be happy to be home alone because he stressed me out. I would go get him on my day off.

One weekend, I went to Shreveport, but when it was time to go back, Red wouldn't answer the phone. I knew he was with a girl. He was also in my car, so I had to wait. When he finally came back, I had to go to the store. I looked at him to ask where he had been, and I see the biggest "RED" and purple passion mark on his neck. Red is a light-skinned dude and couldn't have covered it up if he wanted to. I said, "So you were fucking last night? You got this big ass passion mark on your neck." He acted as if he didn't know it was there and made a big show of looking in the mirror himself. When he saw it, the fool said, "That ain't no passion mark!" I thought, really Red? I might play the fool with you, but I'm not a fool. I said, "Let me drop your ass off cause I'm about to go back to Texas, and your ass is not coming!" I was mad and hurt. I was so mad I couldn't even ıss him out. I dropped his ass off and headed back to ɛxas. He was calling and texting, but I didn't answer. I was ıst trying to make it home safely.

I got home, took a bath, and took something to help ιe sleep. I got up and went to work. I told my friend from ′ork what he did. Red was wrong for that. If you're going to heat, don't let the female put a passion mark on your neck, ummy. I let some days go by before I even texted him back. Ie was saying how sorry he was and that he and the girl, hat put the passion mark on his neck, didn't have sex. He ̣laimed she had done it in the club. He thought I was stupid, ̣ut I didn't believe that shit. It went in one ear and came out he other.

It was about a week later before I went back to ¡hreveport. Red begged me to come see him. I did, and the ̣assion mark was still on the fool's neck.

I got mad all over again. He kept saying, "I'm sorry. It ⱴill never happen again." He asked for another chance, and thought I was in love with him, so I said okay.

That night, we went to the movies and I began hinking about my cycle and why it has not come yet. My stomach was cramping like it was going to start, but I am never late. I told Red that when we left the movie, I needed to go to a store to buy a pregnancy test. We got one, and I went to my mom's house and took the test. Nervously, I waited the three minutes. When I saw "pregnant" pop up, I instantly started feeling sick. I texted Red and told him that was pregnant again. He said I should have just kept the other baby. It had only been about three or four months since I'd had the abortion. I was so disappointed in myself for getting pregnant again, and it was embarrassing, too.

I was just about to start a new job in Texas. It was not the right time for me to be pregnant. I know that when I'm pregnant, I become too sick to function. All I want to do is eat and sleep. I just couldn't work pregnant.

I didn't want to tell anybody. I felt ashamed, so I waited. I started the new job sick and all. I tried my best to go every day. I would be at work throwing up. They didn't want you to miss any days for the first three months. I was fucked because I was too sick after about two weeks. I couldn't do it. I didn't go back. Red said some hurtful shit, and was so mean to me, because he was so mad at me. That

ade me just lie in bed and cry. He said he was going to
ove back to Shreveport. I was broke, and he was too. He
lled and asked his mom for some money. She sent him
me money that day. I was so hungry, and Red said,
Damn, you can't go a day without eating?" He hurt my
elings so bad. I was pregnant with his baby, and he didn't
ant me to eat? I went to my brother's house and told them
was pregnant again. I cried and told them how mean Red
as to me. I told them I couldn't have this baby, I couldn't
o to work, and that I quit because I was too sick.

That night, I was so depressed and overwhelmed that
wanted to die. I took an overdose, and I called and told my
nom. She called my brother, and he came and took me to
he hospital. They gave me this black chalk stuff to drink. I
ept throwing up. They asked was I getting abused at home.
should've said, "Yes, mentally abused by Red." But
nstead, I said, "No." Though my brother was with me the
whole time, Red came later. Even in the hospital, he was
nean to me when my brother stepped out. He kept saying
e was ready to go. My brother left after a couple of hours. I
lidn't want him to leave me with Red. Red was so mean to

me once they discharged me, he didn't even talk to me on the way home.

The next day, Red wouldn't even go to the store to get me a Sprite to drink or anything to eat. My brother told my mom I was pregnant again, so now she knew. She wanted me to come back home, and I wanted to go back home also. needed to be around someone who loved me and who wasn't so mean to me.

That day, Red and I got into it really badly. We had a fight, and he took my keys to my car and tried to leave. I was so pissed that I busted my window out of my car with my hand. My hand was cut up, but I didn't feel it. I was too mad. He still left in my car, and I called the police on him. It took the police hours to come. My brother came and waited with me until they arrived. He was upset, but my brother was too cool. He would just sit back and watch what happened before doing something. I'm sure he knew I was going to be back with Red eventually. Hours later, the police came. I told them what happened and that he had taken my car.

They did the police report, and after that, I left with my brother and went to his house. I was so sad, but my brother and his wife made me feel comfortable at their house. I called Red's mom, told her what had happened, and told her that I was pregnant. She told me not to have the baby because Red didn't need any more kids. I wasn't planning on having the baby anyway. Red finally called the next day and told me to come get my car from his friend's house. My brother took me over there.

Around this time, Red had made his way back to Shreveport. He knew I had called the law on him, so he wanted to get out of Texas. I got my car and went to my house. I cried and cried, so I decided to go to my mom's house in Shreveport. When I got there, I cried on my mom's shoulders. She told me everything would be alright. When my mom told me that, it made me feel better; it always has. I ended up dropping the charges against Red so that he would stop being mad at me.

My plan was to get an abortion, go back to Texas, and find me another job. The only problem was, I was broke, and Red was too. I asked my brother if he could give me half of the money, and he did. When I went to the abortion clinic, they did an ultrasound. I was about thirteen weeks along. I told them I wasn't working, so they took almost two hundred dollars off the fee. I would have to pay four hundred dollars, but I had to get it done ASAP, because I was almost four months pregnant. I knew this abortion was going be the hardest because, when they did the ultrasound I saw the baby. The baby was big, too. I thought, damn, if I kill this baby, then without a doubt, I'm going to hell! I knew if I killed this baby, this was going to haunt me the rest of my life. Red was supposed to give me the other half of the money on the day of my appointment, but he didn't. I cried and was upset, but I just thought, well I guess I'm having a baby. This was what Red wanted. I guess he thought I was going to put up with his shit forever since I was having his baby.

Once I decided I was having the baby, I started looking for me a doctor. I found one when I was right at fifteen or sixteen weeks, and that same day, I found out it was a girl. I was happy, but I would have preferred a boy.

ed wasn't so happy because he only had one boy and lready had three girls.

When I got home, my mom and sister asked what the aby was. I said, "It's a GIRL!!!!!!"

I was happy but also sad because I knew Red wasn't oing be much help to me. I had already seen how he was vith his other kids.

It seemed like once I had decided I was keeping the aby, Red started showing his ass. Days before my birthday, ted had my car towed. I tried my best to keep it from my nom, but my car was in her name, so she found out nyway. I couldn't get the car out without her. Red gave me he money to get my car out, and when I did, I found a girl's air, panties, bra, driver's license, and belt. I was livid and urt, and I wanted to fuck Red up. I should've, but I was regnant, and didn't have the energy. That was a fucked up irthday!!!!!

After that happened, my mom made me stop letting ted drive my car. This was fine with me because he was very wrong for fucking a girl in my car.

***

Throughout my whole pregnancy, I cried a lot and was depressed. I didn't go anywhere. I just stayed in the house and only went to my doctor's appointments. I hated being pregnant by Red. He went to a couple of my doctor appointments with me, but Red always had a way of fuckin up my mood. He was so stupid; I didn't care about going to my doctor appointments by myself.

During my pregnancy, I prayed and cried a lot. I prayed that God would give me the strength to leave Red alone once I had the baby. I didn't want to be holding my baby and crying over her daddy. I just couldn't do that.

I also was worried that the baby wasn't going to have anything. I wasn't working, therefore, I was broke. Red wasn't working either and was broke most of the time. My mom kept telling me to stop worrying, but it was hard not to.

She threw me a baby shower and a lot of my family and friends came. They blessed me with almost everything the baby was going to need. My brother bought a lot of things too. My baby girl had plenty of stuff, and that took a lot of the worrying away. God is GOOD!

During this time, Red ended up going to jail for some reason. I was just a little sad but not much. In a way, it was a relief to me. Most of the times he would call from jail, I didn't answer. I didn't want to hear the shit he had to say because even from jail, he would be pissing me off. My due date was in January, and he went to jail around November. I was hoping that he would be out when I had the baby, and that's about it. He did about a month in jail, and close to Christmas, he got out. I was happy, I guess. I was just ready to have the baby.

January came, and I was trying my best to get my doctor to make her come early, but he wouldn't. I was tired of being pregnant, and I was so fat. I was over it!

January 25th, 2012, my baby girl was born. Red came to the hospital drunk and walked into my room right as I was pushing the baby out. At least he came, I guess! She came out looking just like Red and my mom. I was happy that she was a healthy baby girl, and I was so glad it was over. Only three people came and saw me in the hospital, my cousin, my son, and his grandmother. No one from Red's family came. That hurt, but it was alright, because I knew they weren't going to be too much help. Hell, Red was barely up there with me. When I got out of the hospital, Red's mom and his kids came to see the baby. I was very surprised because Red was missing in action. He didn't see the baby until days later after we arrived home.

Red showed me that he wasn't going to be there. What he didn't know, was that I was still praying that I would be able to leave him for good. Red was still cheating and playing all types of games. He was staying with his home boy not too far from me. The baby was about two or three months old when we got into a really bad argument. He was talking so much shit to me and was saying that he didn't care about the baby. I got in my car, left the baby with my mom, and headed to where Red was living. He said that he wasn't there, but I wanted to see for myself.

When I got out the car, I saw his homeboy. I asked if Red was there, and he said he didn't know. As he was walking in, I followed him. I went to Red's room. He wasn't there, but on his bed, that I had given to him, I saw a girl's clothes and shoes. It looked like she had been staying the night. I was LIVID! I looked around, and I came across a

ottle of bleach that had not been opened. I said to myself, I
now how to get him where it hurts. Red loved his clothes
nd shoes. I got the bleach and started pouring it all on his
othes, shoes, hats, and also on her clothes she had on the
ed. I poured it on the bed, too. I didn't stop 'til the bleach
was gone.

Then his home boy said in a sweet voice, "MiMi, you
ot to go." I said, "Okay, I'm done!" I felt good. I know
hat's crazy, but it was payback for all the shit this man had
one to me and his baby. I had a smile on my face the whole
way home. I knew that was going to make him mad. Red
oved his clothes, but now he was going to have to buy new
hit because I bleached all his shit. He called me. I told him I
ad been by his house and that he would see when he got
here. Then he called his homeboy, and his homeboy told
im what I did!

Red called me saying that I would pay for his clothes.
He was talking shit, but I was laughing. Payback's a bitch,
uh?

I went back home like nothing had happened. My
mom didn't know what I had just done. I checked on the

baby and went to sleep happy that night. I did feel a little bad that I allowed this man to get me out of character. I know that I would not have normally behaved in this manner, but I still wasn't going to replace his shit.

I started looking for me a job. I was tired of asking Red for money or telling him what the baby needed.

When the baby was six months old, I told Red that I was done, and I meant that. We didn't have sex anymore or anything. I was done with Red. Yes, it was hard, but I had help. I had two dudes that helped me get over him.

Derrick came in my life when I was working stacking magazine shelves. He was checking me out, and I was checking him out. Finally, he said something to me, and that's when it started. I liked Derrick. He was handsome and tall, and he had a good job. The only problem was that he had a girlfriend. I didn't care, though. I had just gotten out of a relationship, so I was just looking for a friend. Derrick and I became good friends.

The first time Derrick and I had sex it was great. He turned me on all the way, and he ate my cat just right. We dn't have sex as much as I would've liked, but when we

d, ooh wee!

I liked Derrick, and he liked me, too. He started

lling me that he loved me and I would say it back. One

eekend, his girlfriend went out of town, so he had the

ouse to himself. I never thought he would invite me over,

ut one day, he asked, and I said, "Yes". He came and

icked me up. I was really in shock. When we got to the

ouse, I saw that it was a nice house. He showed me around,

nd he showed me all the pictures of them and the kids that

ere around the house. I started to feel a little bad. We went

n his man cave room. We talked and watched a little TV,

en he said, "Come with me." He grabbed my hand, and I

t him lead the way. We went in the extra room, and he laid

ne down. He pulled my pants and panties down; then he

tarted to eat my cat. I was still thinking about what we were

oing in their house. We fucked, and it was good; the sex

as always good with Derrick.

After we had sex, we went back to his man cave. I

ould see that he felt bad, too. We both knew we were

wrong. I had never messed with anyone in the home they

shared with their girlfriend, nor have I had sex with anyone in the home they shared together. After that day, we still talked, but we didn't have sex for about a week.

My sister told me she ran across a dude that I was crazy about when I was young, and he had asked about me. He gave my sister his number to give to me. When she told me, I had so many feelings come back. Rod and I went way back. I had messed around with him when I was fourteen. At my age, his dick was so big, it sent me to the hospital. I was peeing blood, and my cat was so swollen. I let my mom see it before I went to the doctor. She asked me if I was getting molested. I said, "No", but how could I tell her I was having sex with a boy that had a huge dick. That was all I could think about when my sister said his name.

I gave him a call anyway, and it was so good talking to him. We had a history. I told him I had a little girl, but I wasn't with her daddy anymore. We had a lot to catch up on.

A couple of days later, we hooked up, went to his house, and had hot sex. His dick was still big, but since I was older, I could take it.

I had these two men in my life, and I liked the sex with both of them. They both satisfied me in different ways. It got to the point that I was fucking every day. One day, it would be Derrick, and the next day, Rod. If it were up to me, we would all be in bed together. I would be laying in the middle of them, fucking them both. Crazy, huh?

I liked both of them when it came to sex. I couldn't tell either one of them about the other, though. They were my boys, and I loved fucking my boys, and they loved fucking me.

Around this time, I was looking for another job. I didn't like doing the magazines anymore because it didn't bring in enough money.

I finally found a job around October of 2012. I liked the job. It wasn't hard, and it was full-time with the weekends off. I was good for the time being.

I was still having sex with both of my boys, but not as much as I would've liked, because both of them would be busy. Around the time I was messing with them, I found out my aunt had cancer. I never even thought about her dying. I thought she would get better. My mother loved her aunt to death, and they looked just alike. My aunt had been with me all of my life, so I couldn't imagine her not being there for my mom. My mother went and visited her a lot in the hospital. TJ and I went with her a couple of times. She loved my baby, and she called her "TJ". Even in all the pain I saw her in, she would still ask for and want to see TJ. My aunt had bone cancer, and it spread all over her body.

She was in a lot of pain. When my mom would visit her, she would just moan. My mom would just hold her hand. I knew she would die one day, but I never thought the day would come so soon. December 28th, 2012, my aunt died, and my mother cried and cried. I felt so sorry for her because I know how much she loved her. I hadn't seen my mom cry like that since my sister and my grandmother died

That was a sad day. I cried, too. All the grandkids cried just from seeing how sad and hurt my mom was. I felt her pain.

On the day of my aunt's funeral, I still couldn't believe she was gone, but when I saw her in that casket, it was real. My mom spoke at the funeral. She did well, and she didn't break down. She was good at first, but then it hit er, and she started to cry. I was already crying. I hated this ay for having to bury my aunt. To know that we would ever see her again, made that another very sad day.

On the way home from the funeral, my good friend alled me and asked if I had heard about Fred. When I said No", she said that he had passed away. She had picked a ucked up day to tell me that. I couldn't even cry because I vas still crying over my aunt. It was all too much for me. I aw Fred's cousin a few weeks before he died, and she was upposed to be getting me his address so I could write him. t had been a long time since I had talked to Fred, but he was lways on my mind. When my friend told me he had died, I vas sad. I just couldn't cry. I didn't attend his funeral ecause I couldn't see Fred like that. I wanted my memory o be of the last time I had seen him. It did fuck me up, hough. I hated it, but I knew he was in a better place. I new that he and my aunt weren't in any more pain!

I took a couple of days off work when all this happened. Derrick and I weren't talking as much; then we topped talking completely, though I would still think about him a lot.

Rod and I were still fucking, and one day, as I was talking to my homegirl, we decide to have a threesome with Rod. That has always been a fantasy of mine. I trusted Rod, so I didn't mind having the threesome with him. When I told him about it, he was down with it. What dude wouldn' be down? We planned the day, and everything went as planned. My friend and I got over there, and I didn't waste anytime drinking. This was new for me, and I needed to be drunk. I got so drunk that night. Rod and my friend were messed up, too. She fell asleep. Rod and I went in the room, and we started fucking. He asked me where was my friend. went to get her, and we all got naked. Rod and my friend's hands were all over me. It was so weird, but I was drunk. We all got in the bed. I started fucking Rod again while my friend watched. After I got off of him, she got on him. She didn't stay on him long because she had a man and Rod's dick was too big.

She didn't want her man to find out. I told her that I understood. Rod started back fucking me, and my friend was just lying there. Then he was touching her cat while he fucked me from behind and she was touching my breast. We

I were fucked up that night. We didn't know what we were doing. That was my first threesome and hers too. Once e came, she put her clothes on. I put a shirt on, and I walked her to the door. It was late, so I told Rod to take me ome in the morning and passed out. Morning came, and I was sick as a dog throwing up nothing but liquor. I sat right n the floor at Rod's house until he was ready to take me ome. My head was hurting, I felt nauseated, and I was just eady to get in the bed. It was a fun night, but maybe too nuch fun. We all enjoyed ourselves, but we never talked bout doing it again.

After the threesome, Rod and I would have sex from me to time. He had things going on, and I was in the rocess of looking for another job. Months later, I was blessed" with a good job working nights and making good noney. I was so happy. Before I was blessed with this job, I ever saw myself being able to move out of my mom's ouse, nor buy a new car, on the salary I was making at my ast job. I was always having car problems, but that job came ight on time. My mom was tired of keeping the baby, so ince I was going to be making more money, I decided to put her in daycare. She would be in daycare during the daytime so I could sleep, and my mom would watch her at night.

At first, everything started out great. That job had me tired, so tired, that I wouldn't even get out of bed. The whole day would pass me by, and I would still be tired. I worked six days a week. So on that one day, I was too tired to do anything. I know I went a couple of months without sex because I was just too tired. At my job, they worked the shit out of us. I would work ten to eleven hours daily with one day off. It was crazy. It didn't bother me at first because I was trying to save money, work on my credit, and buy the things my kids needed. But after a while, I stopped being able to sleep. I would wake up all through the day. This went on for months until I started to get depressed. One day at work, I had an anxiety attack. The attack was brought on by lack of sleep while trying to work, take care of a one-year old toddler, and my son who came over on the weekends. During the week he stayed with his grandparents.

I began to get mentally and physically sick. I went to my doctor, and he gave me two weeks off. I needed it.

During my time off from work, my mom and I weren't getting along. I can't even remember why, but I do remember that I went to her room to tell her something, she napped. She said that if I didn't get out of her face, she would BLOW MY BRAINS OUT! She even started looking for her gun. I went back to my room and sat on my bed crying. I knew that I didn't really make her mad enough where she would want to kill me, but as I sat on my bed, she came in my room, and I said, "Do me a favor, and kill me!" I didn't care. I was tired. She looked at me, then walked out and went back in her room. Now, part of me thinks, my mom would have shot me. But I also knew that my mother had a mental illness as well, so if she would have, I think it would've been the illness that made her do it. I knew my mother loved me and would never do anything to hurt me. That same day, I went to the doctor, and I told him what my mother did. He told me he would have to call the police. I begged him not to. I told him that if he did, it would make it worse, and my mom would put me out. I begged my doctor not to call the police, but he kept saying that he was. I left mad and nervous because I knew my mom would be mad as hell. So when I got home, I was scared to tell her, but I went ahead and told her that I had told my doctor. I told her that wasn't thinking that he was going to have to report it. She was mad, and she started putting on her clothes like she was about to go. I told her I wasn't trying to get her in trouble, but she was mad, and she said I had to go. I left and went to my sister's house. I had to tell my doctor that I wasn't at my mom's house anymore and that I would be at my sister's house. After that, he agreed not to call the police. That was a big relief because if she would have gone to jail or the mental hospital, she probably wouldn't have talked to me for a long time.

I stayed at my sister's house for about four days, and I was so ready to go. I liked being at home, so I called my mom and asked if I could come back home, and she said yes. I think I flew home. A week later, I went back to work because I felt a lot better. I still wasn't sleeping that good, but the two weeks I was off allowed me to catch up on some sleep.

Not long after I returned to work, I started having problems at my job with a co-worker and the supervisor.

hey were stressing me the fuck out. I really had changed
ny ways, but the people up there were about to make me go
ack to the old me, a person I try to keep on lock, so I really
ad to pray hard. I had just got blessed with a new car, and
he devil was about to make me lose my job. I would have if
would've gone back to the old me, but thank God, I kept it
ogether and didn't let the Devil win. He almost did, though.
After my co-worker and I go into it, the supervisor started
arassing me. I was called to the office damn near every day.
he harassed me about little things like my pants or my
hoes. She was pushing it, so I filed harassment on her. They
noved me away from her, and that was the best thing for
ne. My one-year contract at my job was coming to a close,
nd I knew they weren't bringing me back. I had already
rayed about it and put it in Gods' hands, so if it was meant
o be, they would bring me back. If not, I was going to leave
nd find me something else. Life goes on. One day, the
upervisor brought me a letter, and it stated that I would not
e returning once I made my year. I couldn't stress about it
ecause I had already prayed about it.

I went home and told my mom. She told me that she knew I could find something, but she didn't think that they would be letting me go. I told her they had already given me the paper. That night when I went to work, my new supervisor came up to me and told me that I would be coming back! She told me to go on my five-day break and informed me when to return! God is GOOD! I went on my break, and after five days, I returned. A lot of people just knew I wasn't coming back, and when they saw me, they thought they had seen a ghost. I walked in rolling my eyes at them.

I was still saving my money and working on my credit, so I decided it was time for me to be back in my own place. I was tired of staying with my mom. We got along, but it was time to go. My mom didn't want me to move, but I didn't care. I started looking around, and I found a house I liked right around the corner from my mom's house in the neighborhood where I grew up. I paid my deposit, and a couple of weeks later, I moved in. I was so happy and proud of myself. I was so blessed and grateful, because, without God, I would've been dead.

Depression, Sex and Death: A Memoir

My move-in day was in May. I had bought all the
uff I was going to need and got everything turned on.

That was the day I met Larry. He came to turn my gas
n, and we started talking as if we had known each other a
ong time. We could relate to each other, and he seemed like
cool, hardworking man. I was hoping that he wasn't
narried or with a girlfriend, but I saw the ring, and he told
ne he was married. I was a little bummed. We kept on
alking about life in general. My mom pulled up, and we
tarted walking back to the front. My mom saw him, and she
old me that he was the type of man I needed, one that
vould work and keep a good job. Before he left, I gave him
ny number, and he smiled. I never told my mom he was
narried. Later on that day, he called, and we had a good
onversation. I hated that he was married because I wasn't
rying to come between him and his wife. We texted a lot.
Ie was always trying to see me, but I wouldn't let him. This
vent on for weeks, and then one night, he said he wanted to
ee me, and I said okay. We talked and stuff, then he said he
vanted to give me a massage. So he took my clothes off and
began to massage my back. Then he moved to my butt, and

he started kissing my ass. He told me to turn around, and I did. My cat was hot and wet. He started kissing my thighs, and then he licked my cat. It felt so good. He knew how to eat cat very well. After that, I was ready to have sex, but he said no. I was shocked, but I wasn't tripping because I knew it would happen one day soon. The very next night, we fucked, and he fucked me right, too.

I was liking Larry. He would bring me food in the morning and give me money. On my off days, we would spend time together and just chill and watch a movie. My little girl liked Larry, too. He would play with her. I know it was wrong for me to be talking to a married man, but I was falling for this man. He would've been perfect for me if he didn't have a wife. He would come to my house in the morning, and we would have sex almost every morning. He was supposed to be working. Well, he was working me alright. Larry and his wife were already having problems before I came along, so he was talking about leaving her. He just didn't know when he would. All I knew was that I was happy with Larry. Some nights, he stayed the night. His wife never even called. I thought that was strange. If my hubby ere out all night, I would be blowing the phone up to see hat the hell he had going on, but she didn't do that. In my pinion, she was doing her own thing. He said that she usted him. I thought, Oh okay. She trusts you, but you and are acting like boyfriend and girlfriend. Larry met a lot of ny friends and my mom. No one knew he was married, nough. I didn't want anybody to judge me because I knew I vas wrong. For my birthday that year, I had a party. He ought me a Michael Kors watch that I had been wanting. hat night, he passed out on my bed. The next morning vhen I got up, Larry had cleaned up my whole house! I was very surprised and glad he did because I was still hung over rom the night before.

Larry showed me that he cared about me, and he started telling me that he loved me. I would say it back because I was falling in love, but it was with a married man. We were both living a lie. I would always tell him that I didn't want to go to hell for our relationship.

Larry asked me to go to Texas with him one weekend, and I went. We had a good time. It was like he was my man and I was his girl. I knew it was wrong, but for a minute, everything felt so right with us. We were able to go out together and not be worried if someone would see him. I wished it could have been like that back home, but it couldn't. We did enjoy our time together in Texas, though. While we were in Texas, we went to a strip club. He was drunk, but I wasn't. When we got back to our room, we had hot sex. That night was the first night he licked my asshole. At first, I thought he was a freak. It felt good, therefore I let him continue, so I guess I was a freak, too. The next day, it was time to go back home. I wished that we could've stayed longer, but we both had to go to work, and he had to get back to the wife and his kids.

On the way home, he was playing with my cat getting me hot. I started touching his dick until he got hard. If there had been a way for me to fuck him while he was driving, we would've had sex the whole way home. We both couldn't wait until we got to my house. As soon as we arrived, I bathed, we watched a little porn, and we had sex. Larry fucked me right every time. I was hooked on having sex with him, and I was falling in love with him. Some days I would get depressed, and he would ask me what was

rong. I told him a lot of things about me, private things. He
would just listen to me, give me advice, tell me I would be
alright, and tell me how much he cared about me.

My father came to town one weekend for a family
reunion. I asked Larry if he would go with me, and he said
yes. It was like he had two families. When we got to the
family reunion, he met my family, my grandmother, my
uncle, my sisters, my dad and my stepmom. Everyone liked
Larry. My grandmother told me she liked him and that he
was a keeper. My dad said the same thing. Larry was a
likable, very outgoing person. He just had a good
personality, and people were able to pick up on that. My
dad said that he hoped Larry would become his son-in-law.
Larry and I looked at each other and laughed. No one knew
the secret we were hiding, and I wanted to keep it that way.
When we were heading home, I told Larry that I didn't like
lying to my family. We knew we were living a lie, and this
lie had me lying to the people I loved, even though I knew I
couldn't tell them the truth.

I tried a couple of times to leave Larry alone, but it
was hard. I was falling in love with him. I just didn't want to

get hurt. He would tell me that he was going to move out, but I didn't believe it. He promised me he wouldn't hurt me on purpose, and I believed him. In the beginning, we hadn't thought that we were going to get this serious. It was happening, though, and we couldn't stop it.

I talked about Larry a lot to my co-workers. He was always on my mind. I would never text him late at night because I knew where he was. That's why he came over every morning. I had to be crazy about him because I even gave him a key to my house. He came and left as he pleased and I was cool with that.

It was all about Larry, but I started wanting him for myself. I never told him to leave his wife, but he had told me he was going to move out, and he did. He showed me where he stayed, but I never went in because he was still trying to get it together.

I was a home person. I liked him being at my house. Once he did move out, we started to go out to eat and things, and he would stay the night more.

Things started to change when Larry started working two jobs. He stopped having time for me. Saturdays had en our day because that was the day that I would be off ork. So when I stopped seeing him on Saturdays and for veral days in a row, it threw me off. Once a man showed e he didn't have time for me, my feelings would change, d that's what happened to Larry and I. He didn't want me stop talking to him, and a part of me didn't either, but I ad to. My feelings for him had changed, and that's all it ok for me to leave Larry alone.

I got my key from him because I was done, and I idn't want him popping up at my house. It was hard ecause he was so nice to me and my little girl liked him, but was time to move on.

We stayed in touch. He would still text me in the mornings. I would reply, but when he would want to come ver, I wouldn't let him.

He was always telling me that he missed me, and I nissed him too, but it was over. I was tired of lying to people about us.

After Larry, I chilled out for a minute. I didn't mess with anyone. When I got horny enough, I would fuck a dude that I had messed with in my past, but for the most part, I was chilling.

I started talking to a dude that worked with me. When he first started, all the girls were talking about him but me. I didn't pay him any mind. Then he started to speak to me, and one morning, he left his number on my car. He was very cute and had a baby face. He started out nice, and didn't want to mess with people I worked with, but I fell in dude's trap.

The first time we had sex, he ate my cat and fucked me, and it was pretty good. After that, we had sex a lot. He would come to my house for his lunch, we would fuck, and he would go back to work.

One day, he asked me if he could stay with me for a little while. I had to think hard on that because I was used to being by myself, and we weren't in a relationship. We were just fucking. For some reason, I felt sorry for him, so I let him stay. It was a bad decision. We fucked a lot, but we didn't get along. He was always mad about something, and he was very hard to please. He would fuck up my mood in my house. I stopped wanting to be at my house because he would fuck up my vibe so quick. He got on my nerves, and I wanted him gone. I just didn't know how to tell the fool.

After about two weeks, he left. He didn't say "thank you" nor give me a dime. I felt played. I had let this fool play me, but would never help him again! I was really happy he was gone!!! He and I were on and off. One minute, he would text and call me and talk to me at work. The next minute, he wouldn't say shit to me. This dude was crazy in my eyes and had issues, but a part of me still felt sorry for him, and I don't know why.

We would still have sex sometimes, but then he started asking me to suck on him. I had told him from the start that I don't suck dick and that I don't cook. I make sure I tell men this. I don't even know why he asked me that. I would never suck on him. I liked him but not that much. So he said until I started sucking dick, he wasn't going to have sex with me anymore. I just said, "OK." I didn't care. I wasn't going to lose any sleep about not having sex with him.

One day at work, we were sitting at the table together. It was almost time for me to go, so as I was about to go clock out. I grabbed his phone and walked out. It was locked so that I couldn't see anything. He wanted me to give his phone back, but I kept walking. My friend from work told me she knew how to unlock it, so we went to the bathroom, and she unlocked it with no problem. I looked at his pictures, and this man had like ten videos of females sucking dick. He must really like getting head. I thought he was a real freak for having all them videos on his phone. I told my friend he was going to be mad, so we left the bathroom, and we clocked out. Before I left, I tried to give him his phone. I was telling him to come out of the break room, but he wouldn't. He started talking shit, so I told him that if he didn't come get his phone, I was going to leave. He didn't come, so I headed home. I made it home. I was there for about twenty minutes. I looked at his phone again and started reading his text messages. I read a message from his ex, and they were still very much in love. They were still telling each other that they loved each other. I wondered why they didn't just get back together, but then I saw in the message where she said how he talked to her bad and that he had a bad attitude. I was outside because I knew he was

ɔming to get that phone. When I saw him pulling up, my
eart dropped because I knew he was pissed. He pulled up
ılking shit. I asked why he and his ex weren't together if
ɪey were still in love. I also asked why he had been lying to
ɪe the whole time. I wasn't tripping about the messages
ɪecause he wasn't my man. I just wanted to know why they
vouldn't get back together. He kept saying, "MiMi, give me
ɪy phone." I said, "Can you please answer my question?"
Ie just kept saying, "Give me my phone." He had gotten
ut of the truck, so I walked around the car. He got back in
till talking shit. He backed up, then put the truck in drive.
ɪhis fool tried to run me over where I was standing in the
ɟrass. If I hadn't moved, I'm sure both of my legs would've
ɪeen broken. I was in shock! I said, "You're going to run me
ɪver? Over a phone? Really?" He said, "Yes. You shouldn't
ɪave taken my phone. We're not together, MiMi." I said,
"Dude, I know that shit. You don't have to tell me that." He
ɪept talking shit, and he had pissed me off by trying to run
ɪver me. Then I saw him looking for something. He grabbed
ɪis gun. I said, "You would shoot me over a phone?!? You
vould really kill me over a phone?!?" He said, "Yes!" I knew

then that I was dealing with a NUT!!! He got out of the truck, and I could see it in his eyes that if I didn't give the man his phone, he would hurt me. So, I handed him his phone. He had me scared. He took the phone and left.

After he left, I was fucked up; I couldn't believe what had just happened. I kept thinking, What if I hadn't moved? What if he would've pulled the trigger? I couldn't believe he had done all that over a phone. He started calling and at first, I wouldn't answer, but he kept calling. I answered. He said, "You shouldn't have taken my phone." I said, "So you were going to kill me and go to jail over a phone?" He said, "Yes, but if I would have hit you with the truck, I would've gotten you up". I knew for sure then that this dude was crazy. He never apologized to me. He just kept saying that I shouldn't have taken his phone. I said, "You're right. My bad." I wasn't trying to lose my life over a phone. I had never thought that he would do all that. He had shown me that morning that he was crazy. My mom had always told me that when a person showed you who they were, believe them. The next day, I didn't even want to see him at work. I wouldn't even look his way. I tried to stay as far away from m as I could. I left him alone after that for a while. We

dn't talk for a minute, and I was fine with that because he

as too crazy for me.

RAY

January came around, and my good friend's little girl's birthday was on the seventeenth. She was turning one so I went to her birthday party. While I was there, my friend's baby girl's father gave me the phone. It was a boy I used to talk to years ago. We had never had sex or anything before. We talked. I gave him my number and told him to call me so I could have his number. He called, and I stored his number in my phone.

We talked later that day, and that night, he came and saw me before I went out. Ray was very handsome, and his voice sounded like that of a little boy. He was cool, but maybe too cool. The next night, he came over, and we talked for hours just getting to know each other. Earlier that day, I was watching a show called Power. That show had made me horny, and we watched some of it while Ray was over there. I was so horny, I could've had sex with him that first night, but I didn't. We waited until the next day. When he came

ver that morning, he ate my cat, and he ate it good, too.
When it was time to have sex, though, he couldn't get hard.
his had never happened to me before, and I started
inking he wasn't attracted to me. He kept telling me that
ick of attraction wasn't the problem. I said, "Well why can't
ou get on hard?" He said he didn't know. I guess he was
oo excited.

He kept trying to get hard, but it didn't happen. He
aid he would try the next day again, and I was cool with
hat. I was so attracted to Ray. There was something about
im that turned me on. The next morning, he came back,
nd we were finally able to have sex. From that day forward,
was hooked on Ray's sex. I wanted to have sex with him all
ay, every day, but we didn't have sex every day. We
tarted out having a lot of sex; then we would go weeks
vithout sex. I was always trying to give him my cat. I fell for
Ray quick. I liked this man, and I would've done anything
or him. Since I had been staying in my house, I had never
ooked for a man. I wanted to cook for Ray, though. That's
ow much I was feeling him. I asked him if he liked steak
ind potatoes, and he said yes. I told him I was going to cook

for him, and I would let him know what day. So when the day came, I went and got everything. I bought him some Hennessy to drink because I remembered he had told me he liked it. My mother came and helped me cook. She took ove and cooked the steak and potatoes and made a salad. She se the table as if we were at a 5-star restaurant and lit a candle. Now all I had to do was hope that Ray came. There was a time when he had told me he was coming and didn't show up, so I was a little nervous that he wasn't going to come. My mom and friend both teased me and said that if he didn't come, they would eat the steak.

He came. He was a little late, but I wasn't tripping because he did come. We ate, and we talked. I really got to know the real Ray. He was telling me how he would do anything for me and that he was feeling me, too. I believed everything Ray said that night, and we ended the night with a kiss. I sure did want to fuck him bad, but he had to go.

Around the time Ray and I were talking, I was depressed on and off. At first, I didn't want to tell him because I thought he wouldn't understand. When I told him he was very understanding, and it shocked me. I was just ad that he didn't think I was crazy. I been called crazy all my life, and I would've hated it if he thought I was crazy.

We started talking about sex and having a threesome. asked him if he'd ever had one. He said no and asked me if d had one. I said yes. I asked if he wanted to have one, and e said he was down with it. I told him I would make it appen. I was so sexually attracted to Ray. I mean, he could ust touch my cat, and I would get wet. Sex was always on ny mind, all day, and every day. Ray turned a switch on in ne that I never knew I had. I always liked sex, but sex vasn't on my mind as it was once I started messing with Ray. I wanted him. My body needed him. I would play with myself and think about him. I was turning into a nymphomaniac. I was unable to control my sexual urge. I vanted sex with Ray all the time.

Even at work, I was thinking about sex, and when I :ouldn't have sex with Ray, I would just play with myself.

Before Ray, I had never sent a man a picture of my cat r made a video of myself. But he brought out the freak in ne, and I sent him both. I couldn't believe I did that, but I vould've done anything he said.

One night, I texted my friend and asked if she was down for a threesome. She said yes. I texted Ray and asked was he down; he said, "Hell yeah." So I bathed and told both of them I would call them after my bath. I called Ray first and told him he could come, then I texted my friend and told her she could come. Ray got there first, and we were talking. Earlier that day, Ray and I had already had hot sex, but it didn't matter. I always wanted his sex. When my friend came, she brought some drinks for us. I drank about three of them quick. I had to be a little tipsy for a threesome and I was after that. We headed to my room. We all got naked, and me and my friend laid on the bed. He started eating my pussy first; then he ate her pussy. Then he told her to turn around. He was standing up, and she was on all fours. He slowly entered her and started hitting her from the back. I was just lying there naked and all. She began to eat my pussy and finger fuck me. It was weird, but I tried to block the weirdness out. She did eat my pussy good for a girl. Ray stopped screwing her and started fucking me. I said to myself, I'm not about to eat no cat. I'm not that damn freaky. HELL NO!

So while he was on top of me fucking me, she was sucking on my breasts. Then I heard her say, "Sit on her face," but I acted as if I didn't hear it. Then Ray said to sit on his face, and I had no problem doing that. I sat on his face while my friend was sucking the hell out of his dick, and he was eating the fuck out of my pussy. Then my damn phone rang. My mom was calling. The first time she called, I didn't answer. Then she called again, and I didn't answer again. Then she texted and told me to come get your baby. I told them that we had to stop and that I had to get the baby. I called my mom a "HATER", and we all laughed. I told them we'd continue it another time. We all put our clothes back on; she left, and he stayed while I went to pick up the baby. I asked him if he had enjoyed himself, and he said he loved it.

He left about six that morning, and when he got home, we were texting. My friend and I were also texting.

It seemed as though everybody had enjoyed themselves. My friend said that Ray had fucked her roughly, and I told her that's how he fucks me too. She said that next time she wanted me to sit on her face, and I said okay. Ray told me that her cat was okay but not good and wet like mines. He said she could suck dick. I told him we were going to have to do it again. I didn't know when, but it was going to happen again. After that night, I couldn't stop thinking about how I had let a girl eat my pussy. I'm not bisexual. I only did it for the threesome. I'm not attracted to girls at all. We just had fun that night.

A couple of weeks after the threesome, I was still not sleeping well, and I was having a lot of anxiety and depression. I was tired of not being able to sleep. I was still trying to go to work and take care of the baby. I was stressed out, and not sleeping was messing me up. I started to hallucinate from being so tired. I was only sleeping three or four hours, and this went on, I know, for about a year.

I was mentally and physically tired. I was tired of being depressed and not sleeping, so one day, I decided to take fourteen pills. I wasn't trying to kill myself. I just needed to sleep. I told this guy what I did. He called and told my mom, and she took me to the hospital. The pills made me sick as a dog, and when they asked if was I trying to kill myself, I told them that I just wanted to sleep. I could understand how MJ felt not being able to sleep.

They decided to send me to the mental part of the hospital, and it was crazy, because it had been seven years since I'd been there. I was doing good until I started working that night job and letting the people at my job stress me out.

I didn't have anyone's number, so I asked my mom if she would give me a couple of people's numbers. At first, I wasn't going to call Ray, but my mom told me that he had been texting and calling, so I waited about two days before I called him. I didn't tell him why I was there. I just told him that I wasn't feeling well and when I got out, I would tell him what had happened. I only told a couple of people that I was there, and two of my friends came and visited me. I didn't want to be seen, but they were just showing me support, and I needed it.

The doctor put me on an antidepressant and some medicine for my anxiety. I still wasn't sleeping, though. I was still waking up all through the night. One day, I was talking to my mom, and she said, "MiMi, you might be bipolar." I said, "Why do you say that?" She said it was because I was on a sex high. So when I saw the doctor, I told him what my mother said, and he laughed. He asked me how old I was and did I have a person that I liked. When I said yes, he said, "Well, that's normal."

I was only in the hospital for three days. He told me that maybe with the medicine, I would be able to sleep better. I'll tell you what, there were some very mentally ill people in there. A lot of people were there due to hearing voices. I thanked God that I didn't hear voices. After the three days, he took me off work for another week. I was still very much depressed. I was trying my best to shake it, but I was crying almost every day. I never stopped praying, though, and I had a lot of people praying for me.

It got so bad that I told my mom that if I didn't start sleeping, I was going to end up killing myself. I was just so tired from not sleeping. I went to a sleep clinic and stayed overnight. They saw that I kept waking up, but they never told me why.

I stayed off work for three weeks, and when it was time to go back, I didn't want to. I was still sick, but I had to go back. I had too many bills to pay. My mom wanted me to quit and move back in with her. I thought about it, but I told her that I would keep praying to get better.

Depression, Sex and Death: A Memoir

Suffering from depression is hell. It's a dark place. You feel all alone, and you see no light. I felt so dead inside; just numb, and so unhappy. I hated feeling like that. I would stay in bed all day and wouldn't play with the baby or spend time with my son. I was dying inside, and no one had a clue. I would still put on clothes. People really thought I had it all together, but they just didn't know I was dying on the inside. Depression doesn't have a certain look. You can't tell if a person is depressed just by looking at them. Depression is an overwhelming sense of numbness and the desire for anything that can help you make it from day to day. Sex is what I used to get through a lot of those days.

I started seeing a counselor. Even she said, how on the outside, I looked as if I was fine. That was just my cover because I was so not together. I needed help. I was tired of crying and always thinking. I couldn't shut my brain off, and I was driving myself crazy. Finally, the medicine started helping me feel a little better, and I started working out and meditating. That helped me with my anxiety and depression.

It was still a constant battle. One day, I would feel okay, and the next day, I would feel down. I was still trying to work nights. Some nights I had to leave because I couldn't stop crying. When I would be depressed, I didn't like being around people at all. People made me nervous due to my anxiety.

During this time, Ray and I were on and off. We would still mess around from time to time. I needed some excitement in my life, so I decided it was time for another threesome. I told Ray, and he was like "BABY, you're the boss!" I told my friend, and she was down. We just had to set a day.

The date was set, and it went as planned. I bathed, and the baby was asleep in my son's room. I thought about sending her to my mom's house, but she was asleep, so I decided just to leave her sleeping.

Ray got there first, and we talked while we waited for my friend. I had told her to bring her sex toys this time. So when she got there, she had her little bag, and we didn't waste any time. We all headed straight to my room, and we got naked.

Depression, Sex and Death: A Memoir

She and I were lying on the bed naked. Ray started ating her cat first, and then, he ate mines. He slid his dick iside my wet cat, and my friend was lying there next to us. he started playing with her cat with her toy. Ray pulled out f me and told my friend to turn around. As I laid on my ack, he slid into her from the back, and then she started ating my cat and playing with my cat with the toy. Ray told er to lie on her back, and he got on top of her. I was lying n the side, and she was still playing with my cat with the oy. He stopped fucking her and started fucking me. I loved he way Ray fucked me. While he was fucking me, she was ouching my breasts and sucking on them. Then Ray said to it on his face, and I did. While he was eating my cat out, she vas sucking his dick. She was sucking it good, too. I heard t. Ray was still eating my cat. I asked if he was ready to um. He asked if I wanted him too, and I said yes. For some eason, I was just ready for it to be over. He got on top of me and started fucking the shit out of me. I asked where he was going to cum. He said he didn't know, so I told him to cum in me. He didn't like cumming in me, but most of the time he would. This time, this dude came all on my cat and thigh.

I said, "Really, Ray? You know I don't like that." I instantly went to the bathroom. I didn't like semen on me at all. I came out of the bathroom, and everyone put on their clothes. I said, "Well, this was fun." My friend agreed, and told her to text me when she got home.

Ray stayed a little bit longer, and we talked and watched TV until he left. After he left, my friend texted me and told me she had made it home. Ray texted me when he got home as well. I got in my bed and played with myself. After I came, I went to sleep.

After that, Ray and I didn't talk as much. I was tired of him always lying to me about coming over. It was hard for me to stop talking to Ray. I really liked him a lot, and I wanted to be with him, but he didn't want me as much I wanted him. We didn't talk for a while, and one day when I tried calling him, I found out he had changed his number. I was missing him, but I was moving on with my life. I thought about him a lot, though. It was the sex with him tha had me. He was a freak, and he brought out the freak in me. I can say that only a couple of dudes bring the freak out in me, and Ray was one of them.

I would never forget him, and I believed that he would never forget me because I had given him his first threesome.

After Ray, my sex drive went all the way down. Sex wasn't on my mind as much. That was one of the side effects from the medicine I was on. That was actually a good thing because my sex drive had been out of control.

I was still dealing with being depressed and the anxiety. I was still missing work and crying a lot. I was still seeing a counselor, and she wanted me to go back to when my sister died. I didn't want to go there. I was still grieving the death of my friend Fred and my aunt. I didn't want to go back to 1997. I told her maybe later, but not right now.

I was still dealing with the stress of my job. My counselor wanted me to find another job, but I was like where would I find another job making what I make at my current job. Yes, I wanted to quit my job. Everything that was happening to me was because of my job. That place had stressed me out, but I couldn't quit. I had never really been a quitter. I felt as if I was at that job for a reason. God had blessed me with that job, and I wasn't going to leave until

GOD said so. I would be there until GOD said I was done, and when He says I'm done, He will bless me with something better! I'm only still here because of GOD. The devil wanted me to kill myself a long time ago, but GOD said, "Live!".

2015 has been a very challenging year, but through my ups and downs, I never lost my faith. I have changed for the better. I don't drink or smoke, and I don't go to clubs. A lot of people say that I have changed. I changed for the good because God has brought me through situations when I could've died. I knew I had to change, because only a fool remains the same. When you know better, you do better.

Everything I went through was all necessary!

This is a poem my mother wrote about me when I was with Mike:

I'm not you

Why do you let that nigga beat on you that way?

And break your $500.00 phone?

Then, call the police... and when they arrive you say nothing is wrong.

Why do you then come home and take a razor to your own skin?

You say it does some kind of release to ease the pain within

Why not just kick that nigga in his nuts and mace him right between his ugly eyes?

And then...call the police, press charges; "Shake it off" and tell that coward bitch goodbye!!!

That's what I would do if I were you. But I'm not you.

The clouds will form words if the universe feels you need them.

Just look up.

For MiMi

Tameisha Moore

This is a poem my mother wrote after my friend Fred was shot:

Bang, Bang, Bang...............

He's supposed to be dead, that was the purpose

Shot 27 times with an A-k 47

Two inches of bone, blown out his leg

but angels flew down immediately from heaven.

He heard the shooter's voice say "yeah" we got him, that dude is dead".

As he lay on the ground, 27 holes in him but not in the heart not in the head.

Bleeding profusely, as his soul tries to get away

25 years old, life flashing before his very eyes

Pain grips his body, he can't move

Jealousy, cruel as the grave, friends telling all those lies.

Still in the hospital seven months later

Paralyzed from the waist down.

A colostomy bag hangs from his side

one arm and hand have no feelings,

Depression, Sex and Death: A Memoir

He wears a frown.

Wondering. "Why didn't I just die?"

No one visits anymore, the money is gone

except this one young lady

with a load of problems of her own.

He sheds tears everyday wondering "why did this have to happen to me".

A fate worse than death is what he faces no walking, running, making love, driving dancing or climbing a tree.

Destined to lay in a bed the rest of his life

Spinal cord torn to pieces, back shattered

Legs so twisted that they look distorted

mind and heart so broken, nothing even matters.

Father, died during his hospital stay

Mother, cracked out, forgot she's got a son

Brother, still in the streets, partying like a rock star

Best friend got weary, left, this is no fun.

But this one young lady with a heart of gold

Visits as often as she can, brokenhearted and all

she loved him when he was up, she stills loves him down

because real love will catch you when you fall.

Now, he knows a decision was made in heaven

to spare his life, the reason, still not known.

God said "Live" and that's what will be

One of his promises is to never leave us alone.

Bang, Bang, Bang..............

Can't change God's word, true indeed

He, me, we can still count him

to love us and supply our every need.

The clouds will form words if the universe feels you need them, just look up.

By Shelia R Moore

For Help...

NAMI: National Alliance on Mental Illness Helpline	(800) 950-NAMI (6264)
National Suicide Prevention Hotline	(800) 273-TALK (8255)
SAMHSA Treatment Referral Helpline	(877) SAMHSA7 (726427)
National Center for Posttraumatic Stress Disorder	(800) 273-8255
U.S. Department of Veterans Affairs Depression and Bipolar Support Alliance	(800) 826-3632
Boys Town National Hotline Crisis hotline that helps parents and children cope with stress and anxiety	(800) 448-3000
Hopeline	(800) 442-HOPE (4673)
Mental Health America For a referral to specific mental health service or support program in your community	(800) 969-NMHA (6642)
National Domestic Violence Hotline	(800) 799-SAFE (7233)
National Sexual Assault Hotline	(800) 656-HOPE (4673)
National Suicide Prevention Hotline	(800) 273-TALK (8255)
Postpartum Support International	(800) 994-4PPD (4773)
PD Moms	(800) 773-6667
S.A.F.E. Alternatives	(800) 366-8288
Cutting Resources	(800) 334-HELP (4357)

95590112R00077

Made in the USA
Lexington, KY
10 August 2018